THE MINISTRY WE NEED.

BY

S. SWEETSER.

"The harvest truly is great, but the laborers are few.

PUBLISHED BY THE
AMERICAN TRACT SOCIETY,
219 WASHINGTON STREET, BOSTON.
HURD AND HOUGHTON, 13 ASTOR PLACE, N. Y.
The Riverside Press, Cambridge, Mass.

RIVERSIDE, CAMBRIDGE:
STEREOTYPED AND PRINTED BY
H. O HOUGHTON AND COMPANY

CONTENTS.

THE MINISTRY WE NEED.

CHAPTER I.

THE WORK.

HE drift of the world is all away from God. This is no novelty. The present age does not differ from other ages in this particular. At one time the worldly forces may be more intense, and the spirit more ardent. The causes which stimulate activity and enterprise have a tendency to give greater energy to ungodliness. Success feeds pride and self-reliance ; and the opportunity for luxury and indulgence enervates the moral character and sensualizes society.

There are reasons for believing that some, if not all these unfavorable processes, are carried forward at the present time with more than usual vigor. If so, it is right to say, that the worldly currents set away from God with an increased momentum. The vital question, always is, how shall men be brought back to God to do his will and enjoy his favor?

If the normal condition of the individual and of

society is one in which God is consciously the central object of affection, and his will the cordial rule of conduct, wherever this moral state does not exist, it is of secondary consequence what the outward aspect of life is.

Civilization is greatly preferable to barbarism; for there are benefits from knowledge, from the arts, from judicious laws, from agreeable conventional usages, which ameliorate the rougher, and enhance the more satisfying circumstances of existence. The way is also prepared for a more hopeful application of higher principles.

On the other hand, barbarism presents more disgusting vices, more violent exercises of the malign passions, with fewer redeeming traits, and withal a discouraging obtuseness of the sensibilities, and a degradation of the mental faculties. And yet, when we weigh the facts touching the relations of society to God, we find a humiliating agreement. In one case men know God, but in their works deny Him. In the other they know not God and establish idols in his place. The idolatry of heathenism is formal and visible. The idolatry of Christendom inscribes no altar with the name of Mammon, institutes no order of worship, while nevertheless it secures that profounder devotion in which with heart and soul, men serve the god of this world.

In its radical significance, then, the problem is one for the whole race of men estranged from God, whether they are polite or rude, whether cultivated or untutored.

If these statements are correct, we cannot resort, with any measure of hope, to those means by which the intellect is furnished or the taste refined. Though ignorance and wickedness are closely allied, taking away the ignorance does not remove the wickedness. Though the highest piety depends upon the aid of knowledge, yet no amount of intellectual training and furnishing will produce piety. History testifies convincingly, that vice ripens under the mellower sky of æsthetic culture, wealth, and intellectual advancement; that the sterner virtues of savage morality decay in the softer climate; and that the absolute decline is sure to hasten to a fatal termination.

The evil cannot be mastered until it is apprehended. If it lies in a moral and spiritual defect; if its source and its energy consist in the alienation of the heart from God, and the indisposition of the will to follow God's counsels, it is clear that no amount of what is called education, no advancement in science, no development and use of the material resources of the world, no refinement of taste, and no courtesies in social intercourse, can be relied on to produce the essential reformation. These things have an inestimable value. They constitute an important part of the world's elevation. Mankind can never reach the high plane on which they are destined to stand without them. But their value depends upon the relation they bear to the moral and spiritual forces which are the efficient reforming powers. They are to be subordinate; to be used as helpers; to come in as the servants of religion. Knowledge is to be urged forward; science, art, literature, commerce, manufactures, all activities and enterprises of which man is capable, and to which the realm over which he has dominion invites, are to receive worthy attention — but they are to be pursued under the control of a mind inspired with love to God, and seeking his glory and human welfare, as its end. Losing sight of this fact is the fatal mistake of many sincere and ardent friends of human progress. These things they ought to do, but not to leave the other undone. They forget the weighter matters of the law.

God has provided adequate means by which the race may be arrested in its departure, and restored to the enjoyment of his favor. The end of divine revelation is the enlightenment, redemption, and renovation of mankind. The world has been slow to see this, for the world by wisdom has not known, nor ever can know God. From the beginning, ingenuity, stimulated as well by pride as by sufferings, has been seeking out some good way. The countless failures, whether of visionary conceits or of thoughtful philosophy, have scarcely abated the ardor or the expectation of the search. It is as true to-day, as it was thousands of years ago, that the world by wisdom knows not God. Science, with its splendid achievements, adds not an iota to the promise. Civilization does not solve the problem; for so far as civilization is moral purification, it is the result of Christianity, and not an element of progress. To whatever quarter the eye has been turned for help, disappointment has been the invariable sequel of unjustified hopes.

So far as the past can furnish wisdom, it declares to us, that the only recovery of man is found in receiving and obeying the truth, revealed by God for our salvation. Any independent and candid examination of the possible forces, by which righteousness and peace can be established, will, with a nearly absolute certainty, lead to the same conclusion. The sword of the Spirit, which is the word of God, is to work deliverance from this moral and spiritual bondage. The gospel of our Lord Jesus is the renovating agency, by which men are to be trained, and qualified to live worthily, and to reach the ample blessings of communion with God. And this is asserted, in the face of all that is claimed for and may justly be ascribed to the influence of increasing and diffused knowledge. It is asserted, notwithstanding the wide range and number of the sciences, so called, whether physical, metaphysical, moral, or social; and notwithstanding the merit due to them, as helpful aids in the formation of a higher social state.

From all these, and every other method, by reason of their inherent inefficiency, we turn to the truth, as unfolded to us by the Spirit of God, made powerful on the conscience and the heart of man by the same Spirit, as the only adequate force, and the only trustworthy discipline, by which the individual soul can be brought back into peaceful relations with God, or the world become subject to his law.

The ministry instituted by Christ is the foremost human agency in applying this method. The work to be done by the ministry, and the weapons to be used, are not indistinctly marked out in the foregoing remarks. The aim is to reconcile revolted men to God; to bring them into loving obedience to his law; to secure to them the divine blessing in its fullness, and so in this life to exalt a fallen race to the felicities of righteousness, and to the pleasures which are at God's right hand, in the life to come.

CHAPTER II.

CONFIDENCE IN THE TRUTH.

N seeking characteristic and essential qualities, needed by those who are to engage in this work, one of the first which attracts our attention is the importance of profound convictions in regard to revealed truth.

When it is remembered that the highest spiritual living we are capable of is prompted by intelligent conceptions of God and his requirements, it will be obvious that to teach and impress the truth of God, must be the substance of a minister's efforts.

A formal knowledge may be sufficient for formal instruction. But the terrible energy of sinful propensity is not restrained by knowledge. It has always been known, perhaps it will never be better known than it has been, that misery is the offspring of vice. And yet the world has rolled on in its career of suffering, unchecked by the demonstration of thousands of years. Some adequate authority is needed to give urgency to the fact, that sin is the forerunner of a fearful doom. This authority is found in the declarations of God, as sovereign and judge. These declarations contain God's purposes, the principles of his government, and the issue of the world's life. They are of necessity the most solemn and weighty truths to which our minds can be given.

As the whole question is one of divine government, the destiny of men depends upon the influence which God's word has upon them. A minister stands between God and his subjects. He bears to them the divine message. He is appointed to utter the threatenings, and to reiterate the promises of mercy. The Scriptures make it clear that eternal life and eternal death are the inevitable issues of preaching. Ministers "are unto God a sweet savor of Christ, in them that are saved, and in them that perish. To the one the savor of death unto death; and to the other, the savor of life unto life."

How now is it possible to enter upon such duties, involving such possibilities, and to discharge them faithfully, unless the minister himself is deeply penetrated with the grand and awful realities, comprised in the truth. A frivolous mind cannot sympathize with the momentous alternatives. An easy credence cannot take in the unmeasured responsibilities. A wavering belief cannot boldly assert the necessary admonition, nor present the infinite fullness of grace in the divine promise. When the intensity of the grasp of sin is considered, the abandonment of the will to the rule of passion, and the insensibility of the depraved heart to spiritual joys, it will be evident, that an earnestness and tenderness, a patience and persistency are needed in pursuing the message of God, which cannot exist without deep and stirring convictions. The advantage is on the other side; for sin has the possession.

In every human view the prospect is a disheartening one. The combined verdict of the world in the centuries of its history is, that happiness is to be found out of God; and to find it, the world has aggregated and expended, with amazing pertinacity, its ingenuity and its zeal. To confront this solid phalanx of opposition requires a just confidence in the resources to be applied. So long as the mind wavers in doubt of the absolute necessity of the gospel; so long as it entertains the thought that the danger is not imminent; so long as it vacillates between the uncompromising claims of God's word and some other possible method of escape, just so long will it be an impossibility to press upon men, with full energy and effectiveness, the demands of God.

A minister, to do his work in any manner corresponding to its importance, should be absolutely possessed and penetrated by the truth. Eternal realities should fill his mind with their august solemnities. His reason, his understanding, his heart, should all be enlisted in the service. The vividness of his own impressions should give vitality to his words. The glow of his heart should impart zeal to his utterance. His faith should inspire confidence in his declarations. Believing with unfaltering firmness, in the word of God, he should speak with unfaltering distinctness whatever comes to him under the sanction of, Thus saith the Lord.

Such a faith is the very substance of sincerity. Sincerity is the soul of true earnestness. Earnestness is the moral power to which the heart yields its readiest obedience. It has proved the triumphant energy in most of the great revolutions of the world. It is the recorded distinction of the most successful preachers from John the Baptist to our day.

Earnestness in error is more convincing than tameness in the truth. Even a simulated earnestness, based upon a professed belief, is more efficacious than a divided heart. Mr. Froude has justly remarked, that "a mind sufficiently in earnest about religion, to prefer truth to falsehood, listens only to teachers who speak with emphasis and certainty, who do not think and say, but feel with warmth and passion. Before a man can persuade others to accept him as a guide, he must know his own mind, and be ready with a Yes *or* No, on the questions with which his hearers are perplexed."

But, for this unadulterated sincerity, for this glowing and mighty earnestness, this prompt and pronounced utterance, it is essential that the mind of the preacher should be fully persuaded, that his heart should suffer no wavering in its convictions of the truth. To him the word of God should be, yea and amen. He should feel, that heaven and earth may pass away, but God's word cannot pass away. He should feel, that the doctrines of the word are as deep laid and as eternal as the throne itself. He should realize, with a conviction as settled as that there is but one sun in the heavens, that there is but one name under heaven given among men, whereby they must be saved. As an ambassador for Christ, he must press men to be reconciled through Him with an assurance as complete as his confidence that the world exists. So long as the word of God is the substance of the argument, the very arsenal of the artillery of a minister, it must be essential to his might and his efficiency, that he cherish profound convictions of the truth; that his own soul be fully under its dominion, and that he speak as one who knows, and by his faith has seen.

This has been a characteristic of God's ministers always. The prophets were wellnigh terrible in their absorbing conviction of the majesty and truth of their messages. The Apostles had a boldness in uttering all the words of the new life, which no authority of rulers, or anger of the populace could withstand. They thoroughly believed what they proclaimed; and confessors and reformers have been men of a like spirit. We can hardly conceive of a successful enunciation of disagreeable and condemning truth without it. It has been the decisive element in the mental and spiritual tone of all great moral renovations, and has left its stamp upon the character and work of the great company of faithful pastors and teachers in the Church of Christ.

We cannot presume that there ever was a time which could dispense with this quality; or that such a time will ever come; most assuredly such is not the case now. For the truth of God is assailed still, with unabated pertinacity. If old issues are abandoned, new ones are started. If some questions concerning the gospel histories are forever settled, and some teachings of the New Testament are established beyond controversy, it does not follow, that skepticism is routed or that unbelief has ceased.

We are to remember that one tendency of our times is to unsettle established beliefs; to disparage the importance of doctrine; to diminish the difference between truth and error; to exalt sentiment, and to proclaim an era of good feeling, with but sparing regard to principles, fundamental in the government of God, as well as in the scheme of redemption. We are to remember that there is a pressure to fix the conclusion, that nothing is to be accepted which cannot be proved, and so become a matter of science. There may be no more danger in this than in the spent or exploded devices and forms of opposition. The point to be noted is, that positive belief in revelation is rejected on the grounds of science; and that faith itself is derided as a source of knowledge. The whole of what is called modern thought, tends to make more imperative in the preachers of righteousness the necessity of carrying with them always into the service of God the unfaltering conviction, that his word is the truth, and that God will not alter the thing that is gone out of his lips.

It is the weakest illusion to assume that a high moral and spiritual life can rest upon feelings and emotions without the force and sustaining efficacy of fundamental principles. These principles are the ground doctrines of the word of God ; and therefore, a needful equipment for a successful and powerful ministry is a profound belief of these truths.

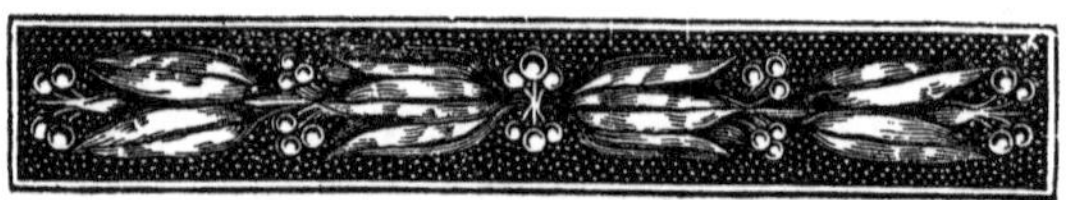

CHAPTER III.

THE LOVE OF CHRIST.

IT should be kept in the foreground that the gospel is a system by itself, amongst what are called religions. Christianity is not the religion of nature, not Judaism, not even pure theism. It is not a code of moral regulations; a digest of wholesome prohibitions and restraints; a compendium of rewards and punishments. Although its morality is the most elevated; its rules of living the purest and most spiritual; its rewards and punishments the most definite and comprehensive; its distinctive quality, over and above all these, is that it is a redemption. It includes every worthy suggestion of natural religion, respecting our duty to God and to man, the practice of righteousness, the cultivation of the virtues, and the condemnation of error and transgression; while it does what no other system can do, in making provision for the recovery, pardon, and salvation of men ruined in their guilt. Preëminently the gospel is not law, but love; while it does not in the slightest degree derogate from sovereignty, it exalts grace; while it diminishes nothing in the condemnation of sin, it delights in the forgiveness of the sinner; while it retains the accuracy of retribution, it glories in the bestowment of a free gift; while it justifies righteousness wherever it can be found, it reinstates in the divine favor and the final inheritance with great joy, every repentant prodigal and every returning wanderer.

To use such a gospel as an instrument, must differ widely from giving instruction in the precepts of the law. It obviously requires the minister to be in sympathy with the spirit of the gospel, or more exactly to be in sympathy with Jesus Himself, the proclaimer of glad tidings. The very name Christianity is not without its significance. It points directly to Christ, as the person who, in his mission and teachings, stands as the originator of Christianity. If, as has been intimated, the spirit of the gospel is peculiar, the distinctive spirit is to be found in Christ. What Christ is — that is the index of the tone and temper of his system. If Christianity is specifically LOVE, it is because Christ in his work is specifically love. It has been truly said, "Christ is Christianity. Detach Christianity from Christ and it vanishes before your eyes into intellectual vapor. Christianity is non-existent apart from Christ: it centres in Christ; it radiates now as at the first from Christ. It is not a mere doctrine bequeathed by Him to a world with which He has ceased to have dealings; it perishes outright when men attempt to abstract it from the living person of its Founder."

It can then hardly be possible to administer heartily

the word of Christ, without feeling and appreciating his love. There is no other avenue to Christ but this. He is never comprehended till his love is understood; and that attainment is never made, until his love has melted, inflamed, and purified the heart. So that a prime quality in the character of a minister, must ever be his lively susceptibility to this love; his spontaneous response to it, and the fervor and zeal with which he is inspired by it.

For it is a defective and unsatisfactory view of a minister's work to present it only as didactic, and ethical; to confine its scope to the inculcation of sound principles, or the culture of the graces which adorn character. No more is it to be looked upon merely as the rebuke of sin, and the utterance of denunciations against iniquity. Whatever tends to withdraw men from the dominion of transgression, to promote righteousness, and to perfect the discipline of a godly life is manifestly within its province.

But when it is remembered that the key-note of the gospel is a proclamation of pardon to men, too deeply insensible both to guilt and danger, that the very mission of Christ was to seek and to save the lost; that his mighty love concentrated itself on this, that men under condemnation might not perish; the pith and substance of the whole work takes another aspect. A minister becomes a messenger of mercy. He is a herald of salvation. He is an ambassador for Christ. He beseeches men in Christ's stead. He pleads with men to be reconciled to God.

As no one can doubt that the moving principle in Christ's humiliation and sufferings was love, so no one can doubt that a sense of this love must be a conspicuous quality in Christ's ministers. It should be a constraining power. Therefore the Apostle says, "The love of Christ constraineth us; because we thus judge, that if one died for all, then were all dead; and that He died for all, that they which live should not henceforth live unto themselves, but unto Him which died for them, and rose again." This is the law of all discipleship.

Its application and its binding force is evinced in the earnest words which follow, describing the ministry of reconciliation. Persuasion, entreaty, beseeching, as though God Himself did through his servants beseech men; these are the exercises by which reconciliation to God through Jesus Christ is sought.

To enter thus into the heart of Christ's mission without sympathy with Him, and without feeling the kindlings of his love and responding to it, must ever be a vain attempt. All the refining, exalting, and stimulating influence of divine love is required to bring about entire consecration to Christ. In such consecration alone can the active powers be devoted to his service. Between a minister and Christ, there should exist a close and peculiar union. How intimate and tender it is, may be inferred from the declaration, "Henceforth I call you not servants, for the servant knoweth not what his Lord doeth; but I have called you friends; for all things that I have heard of my Father I have made known unto you." Without appropriating so much of this passage as belongs exclusively to the immediate disciples, we may safely gather the fact, that those in the work of the Redeemer are admitted to special privileges of friendship and intimacy. It is no mere formality to be Christ's minister. It is not an office, to be fulfilled by perfunctory performances. It is not following a ritual in worshipful observances, or discharging with a cold conscientiousness a round of religious teachings and duties. All such are sacrifices laid upon the altar with no flame to send the acceptable incense heavenward.

There can be no true devotion to God or man without love. And if the law is emphatically binding upon ministers, to be so constrained by the love of Christ as to live to Him and not to themselves, it becomes a question of momentous weight, what is the import and extent of the implied consecration? Can it be anything short of taking the cause of Christ to be one's own; the interests of Christ, his work, his end, to be the interest, the work, and the end of his servants? Is there not of necessity implied an identification of the minister with Christ, such that there shall be but one aim and purpose to them both; so that no one thus pledged to Christ can in any other sense pursue his own ends than as Christ's ends have become his? This will bring the whole energy of the man into the work of God.

For everywhere it is observable that, for the highest human efficiency, there must be an inward, vital, spontaneous movement of the soul towards a chosen object; some idea, some passion, the longing for some achievement, must possess it, inspire it, magnetize it, marshal its powers, sustain it under the toil of striving, during the delay of obstructions, against the depression of partial defeats, and hold it up to endure and persevere, till the triumph is reached. Thus, the searcher for truth, the explorer, the inventor of complicated mechanical contrivances, the patriot burning with zeal for his country's salvation, the prophet glowing with a divine afflatus, as he sees afar the coming glory; the reformer as he confronts the stake, and defies the despotic rage which bars his progress; these and all others who win great victories in great struggles, are moved by concentrated desires and purposes, and are held under the league and conspiracy of the affections and the will, and so are enabled to combine all their energies upon the determination of their noble endeavor. So the Apostle felt, when he declared, "Woe is unto me, if I preach not the gospel." A necessity was laid upon him. So felt the prophet. "His word was in mine heart a burning fire shut up in my bones." He could not withstand the mighty impulse.

Now Christ's work being preëminently and distinctively a work of love, to enter into it with all the heart, demands that Christ's love shall penetrate and pervade the soul, subjecting to Christ the powers and passions of the mind, kindling so responsive a gratitude that the utmost service shall be a joyful offering upon his altar. To have felt the redeeming energy of this love; to have been inspired by it with a good hope of mercy; to have received from it strength for duty and temptation, and to have read in it the assurance of the final glory, serve, most effectually, to purge out the leaven of selfishness, and to allay the fires of an earthly ambition.

There is no loyalty like this, when the soul is bound to the Master by his all-constraining love. It makes it possible to do the work of Christ, as one's own work, and so, to perform it with all the freedom, the heartiness, the joyousness, and the singleness of desire and purpose with which men pursue the objects of their personal interest.

This is a condition of the service of the highest importance. It strips the ministry of the repulsiveness of toil, of the irksomeness of duty and makes it a delight. It lifts it above mercenary considerations and private and personal ends, and invests it with the charm and power of spontaneousness. It unites the servant with the Master in the tender associations and sweet intercourse of friendship, and makes the Lord and his disciples, fellow workers, and sharers together in the tribulation and triumphs of his kingdom.

This responsive affection, this grateful submission of everything to Christ, this hearty adoption of his cause, this self-consecration to all its interests, this surrender of self to the exposures, struggles, and final exaltation of the gospel, should be held not only to be a reasonable, but an essential element in ministerial character. It will give a distinctive tone to the ministry, sanctify and elevate the office, and vindicate for it the appellation of the ministry of Christ.

CHAPTER IV.

GOOD-WILL TO MEN.

O say that the ministers of Christ should be actuated by a principle of good-will to men, is hardly saying more than that the servant should adopt the principles of the master. If it is included in this statement, that the servant should be as his master, it is sufficiently comprehensive. There is little danger of exaggerating the quality of divine love, as it seeks the welfare of the human family. God so loved the world as to send his Son. The Son so loved the world as to give Himself freely to humiliation and suffering for its redemption. The glory of the cross infinitely transcends its ignominy; for it shines and blazes with the effulgence of God's love. The great transaction, elevated above all other events in the world's history, was conceived in the heart of God before the world was; and through it the Infinite Father pours out his heart for his ruined children. Glory to God, and good-will to men, is the wonderful harmony of that scene, which will draw to it the eyes of the universe, and inspire the anthems of eternity.

The Apostle determined to preach, as his one

theme, Christ Jesus, and Him crucified. But to preach Christ crucified, is to proclaim the way of life, by God's love to lost sinners. The cross is the energy of love, because it makes practicable the longings of love. What then is a herald of the cross, but a messenger of good-will to men? And who can so fitly bear glad tidings, as those whose hearts thrill responsive to the joyous theme?

Among the motives urging to the ministry, this should be distinct — good-will towards men; a yearning of heart, to advance welfare and promote happiness. Fairly to put this desire within the sphere of Christian motives, it should be a zeal, kindled by the love of Christ, to secure to men the benefits of the mission of Christ.

To distinguish a Christ-like benevolence from other generous dispositions, is not an unworthy fastidiousness. The object of the ministry is not merely to do good, but to accomplish the peculiar and transcendent good aimed at in the gospel of grace. There are reformations, and ameliorations of evil of value in their sphere, which fall far short of the blessings of evangelical righteousness. There are benefits worthily labored for, which are not the preparation for the kingdom of heaven. There is an enthusiasm for humanity, which may be kindled in a human heart not touched by the Spirit of God, the fruits of which, though precious and lovely to the eye, will not adorn the celestial paradise.

It is not necessary to depreciate the lower forms

of benevolence, in order to give just exaltation to the higher. Ample credit should be allowed to every kind and generous feeling which seeks to lift burdens; alleviate sorrows; to purify society, and diffuse happiness. Whoever in honesty of good-will diminishes the sighs and groans of the world, and adds one ray to the beam of light which irradiates its darkness, is to be welcomed as a benefactor. But the minister of Christ stands upon a higher plane than the highest of human benefactors. He is the messenger of his mercy, who shed his blood for the remission of sins; who died, the just for the unjust, that He might bring them unto God. The scope of this benevolence ranges far beyond the annoyances and ills of a brief mortality. It embraces a blessedness excelling all possibilities of earthly comfort. No conception of the gospel promise is adequate, which does not include the forgiveness of sin, and by it, the redemption of the soul from death, the favor of God, and with it, the crown of glory which fadeth not away.

When it is said, that a minister should be moved by a spirit of good-will, it is meant, that just such love as filled the bosom of the Saviour should inflame him; that just such blessings as Christ purchased by his death, he yearns to convey to men. It means, that he is so in harmony with Christ in his heart, that he burns with desire to persuade men to be reconciled to God, through the blood of the Lamb. How exalted this benevolence is; how different from the ordinary exercises of good-will; how distinct will be the efforts to which it impels, how immeasurable the blessings to which it invites, is readily seen. It is indeed only saying that in every minister of Christ the spirit of Christ should be enthroned. Such benevolence will give the true tone and dignity to the ministry. It will be to it a safe and pure inspiration. It will inflame the preacher with a zeal according to knowledge. It will render him forgetful of self in his regard for others. It will secure him against the enticements of pride and the flatteries of the world. The absorbing worth of the end he seeks will exclude the thoughts of his own instrumentality; and his loyalty to his Master will induce him to lay all the honors at his feet. For love is truly humble, and they who most love the Lord and are most absorbed by the perception and power of his love, are ever the most willing and joyful in carrying out his plans.

If there is any thing real in the union of the believer with Christ, it can never be doubted that those who are especially called to declare his mercy should be eminently moved by good-will to men; that they should be fired with the zeal of the Master, who esteemed not his life dear unto Him, but was straitened until by his death his great purpose was fulfilled.

CHAPTER V.

CHRIST-LIKE COMPASSION.

T may seem that what is conveyed by the term compassion, is properly included in what has already been said. There are, however, reasons for the distinction — a reason of emphasis, if no other.

A portrait of Jesus, in which his compassion is not delineated, does not satisfy. His love takes that form when the sufferings of men arrest his attention. Distress penetrates his heart; sorrow brings tears to his eyes; the cry of the suppliant awakens his sympathy, and the forlorn and helpless hear Him saying, "Be of good cheer, go in peace." His sensitiveness, his appreciation of human necessities, the yearning tenderness which poured out the pathetic lamentation over Jerusalem, indicate the depth and quickness of his compassions. Whatever in Christ illustrates his desire to forgive sin and deliver from the bondage of death, is the working of the same spirit. It is a faithful description of his life and mission, to say, "He had compassion on them, forgave their sins, and healed their diseases."

This quality of the Master's work should be closely

emulated by the servant. It will bring him into immediate contact with the sufferings which the gospel is to relieve. Christ came not to call the righteous, but sinners to repentance, — emphatically *lost sinners.* Christ offered Himself to save the lost. He understood the contents of this fearful epithet. His compassions glowed, and his love yearned over souls under just such a weight of misery. The contumelies He endured in his earthly career, the incomprehensible struggle of Gethsemane, the awful darkness and desertion of the cross, give some glimpses, at least, of his estimate of the woes impending over the guilty. How else could He have ransomed them at such a cost? And how could He have met the demands of the mighty enterprise of love, had not a divine compassion moved Him in it to lay down his life?

It is difficult to frame any consistent interpretation of the life and crucifixion of our Lord, without estimating the guilt of sin as so heavy as to entail a heavy doom of suffering; and therefore counting deliverance from it so great an event as to justify the priceless ransom. No other view can save the cross from the satire of being "a grand impertinence," or exempt the songs of the redeemed in heaven from the charge of heartless exaggerations.

The record we have of the teachings, the mighty and the benevolent works of the Saviour, and the substance of his promises, all imply that sinners in their sins are sufferers, exposed to a retribution, both certain and dreadful. It was this condition of the race under the just administration of God, to which the compassions of Christ responded. Here was a prospect on which the Son of man could not look without the deepest emotion. Nor was it mere emotion; it stirred that current of active love that bore Him through the self-denials and pangs which wrought salvation.

It is a distinct part of the ministerial spirit, to be in sympathy with Christ in his compassions. The servant should know the work he has to do, and in his measure fathom its conditions and its results. He, like the Lord Himself, is to look upon men as lost, and, in the fearful conception of the impending ruin, to be moved for their rescue and yearn for their salvation. It requires the utmost tenderness to deal with the ruined who are insensible to their exposures. Their ignorance and unconcern call for knowledge and compassion in their deliverers. It was because the Apostle knew the terrors of the Lord, that he so earnestly persuaded men to be reconciled to God. The judgments of God hanging over the guilty, were the fittest stimulants to that energy and tenderness which Paul always displayed in his exhortations and appeals.

No one thing is of higher moment in a minister. Without it zeal is apt to be an intemperate and unreasonable heat. Instead, the minister should burn with a fervor justified by his conception of the momentous issue. So long as to him sin is under the condemnation of God, and retribution in the future a revealed fact, so long he has just cause to be in earnest, to plead, exhort with all long suffering and doctrine, and to be zealous in importuning men to accept the mercy of the gospel.

To such a fervor Guizot attributes much of the success of the efforts for the revival of religion in France. He calls it "the passionate desire to save human souls." "A force born and developed in the bosom of the Christian religion, and in that alone." "The ardent solicitude for the eternal welfare of human souls, the never wearying effort to prepare human souls for eternity, to set them, even during this existence, in intimate relations with God, and to prepare them to undergo his judgments; we have in all this a fact essentially Christian, one of the sublimest characterstics of Christianity."

These are pregnant words. They present a vital topic for Christian thought. The passion for souls is distinct from the impulses of humanity. It regards man, and is moved for him as immortal, and as a subject of the divine government. It seizes upon the relations of the soul to God, and the preparation of the soul to meet God's judgment, as facts of the deepest significance. It expands the happiness of man into the limitless future, and grounds the security of that happiness upon enjoying God's approbation.

All true Christian compassion contains this element. It is something more than human instinct. Its scope is broader than the field of temporal wretchedness. It turns upon a more fundamental view of man, than that which embraces only his relation to present scenes and events. Its object is man, in the entireness of his being and possibilities; man in his condition of present and impending wretchedness.

If it degrades the idea of Christ's compassion, to limit it to a tender feeling for the bodily sufferings, under which men labor, it equally degrades the same sentiment in us, if we only sympathize in the brief pains and sorrows of those whose miseries we witness. The mystery of the cross is not relieved by narrowing the force of it to what it may accomplish in our present short existence. On the contrary, such a view exposes it to all the disparaging criticism, so freely indulged in, by those who do not realize the necessity of a scheme of reconciliation.

Christian earnestness is justified by the same considerations which justify the death of Christ. If the cross means that sinners must perish without it, then Christ's compassion means that his heart is moved by the peril of souls exposed on account of sin. If those who are to do the work of Christ need to be moved with feelings like his, the substance of their compassion must be a deep and tender solicitude for the soul.

Christianity is nowhere more distinct from humanity than here; and nowhere is the difference between religious enthusiasm and philanthropy more palpable. The aim of the gospel is, first, to set men right with God; and having done that, the mightiest barrier to happiness is removed. But the controversy with God is in reference to his law. Sin and obedience are the great facts. God's disapprobation follows transgression; and it is reasonable to ask the question, Can an accountable moral being be happy under the government of God, while sin remains unforgiven? If not, then to what purpose are all ameliorating circumstances and mitigations of evil? If the displeasure of God rests upon the soul for its sins, whatever may be the alleviations of the temporal condition, the attainment of blessedness remains an impossibility.

If the present life is the period in which the pardon of sin is to be secured, then the present life has, as opportunity, a value as immeasurable as eternity. The manifestation of Christ in time, then becomes the highest demonstration of divine love. Then the compassion of Christ has a depth, a reasonableness, and a breadth of comprehension, which will be revealed more and more, throughout the ages of eternity, to every redeemed spirit. We can understand something of his willingness to suffer. Though we may not fathom the love which so meekly and majestically exalts the life of the Son of God, we may catch some glimpses of the heart of compassion, which bore the load of human woes. Beneath the lively sympathy He felt for every mortal ill, there was a deeper tone of love — the love of Christ for the soul, which is to survive the body, and which is invested with the capacity to enjoy forever the presence of God, and to be made partaker of the divine nature.

The revelation of this love is the singular revelation made in the Incarnation. To share in this love is the highest gift of God to man. This love, when they caught the idea of it, before it was made actual, filled the heavenly host with amazement. The fruit of it will be the abounding joy of heaven. Any lower view than this dims the lustre of the gospel, and diminishes the glory of the cross. The compassion of Christ sinks to a feeble sentiment, instead of being a divine energy, compassing and accomplishing the exaltation of a ruined race.

When the ministers of Christ assume to carry forward his work, they need the inspiration of this spirit. The aim of Christianity is nothing less than the aim of Christ. The preachers of Christianity must thus expand their view to the same comprehensive limits; and when they preach, preach to men, under the stirring conviction of their real exposures. Nor is it enough to admit the speculative fact of their exposure. This fact must exert its influence upon their hearts. It is the chief fact to excite those melting and resistless compassions that urge ministers to be importunate in their expostulations. Reading the evil of sin in the cross, and the profound dangers of men in the life and death of the Redeemer, they will feel their hearts burning within them; and their desires will be fervent and strong; and they will be impelled to plead with all the force and persistency of intense concern.

It is reasonable to conclude that the strength of active compassion will, in some measure, correspond with the idea entertained of sin. For if the chief peril is found in the impending consequences of transgression, we must intelligently apprehend the transgression before we can be moved by the calamities it threatens.

Precisely at this point does the Scriptural line of thought diverge from the speculative. The tendency of human judgment is to measure sin by the evils or injuries which flow from it, or stand connected with it. Sin and evil come to be synonymous. The guilt of a theft is the injury inflicted. The crime of drunkenness is the swift following wretchedness. Confining, either really or practically, the contents of sin to these narrow limits, eliminates all the spiritual quality of it; gradually absolves the criminal of guilt, and consigns him to the category of unfortunates. The sense of ill-desert vanishes; the idea of resisted authority is lost sight of; commiseration is felt instead of condemnation; and whatever is included in the fearful threatening of God's displeasure ceases to have force.

It is difficult to conceive of any deep moral earnestness being awakened, to deliver men from sin under such views. The ravages of sin have been always present, and have embittered the lives of all the generations of men; and yet no thorough, deep working compassion has ever been elicited; no energetic redemptive scheme has ever been devised.

These, and all feeble conceptions of sin, hide its deadliness and its hideousness by veiling its true nature. The malignity of the will that chooses wrong; the badness of the heart that takes delight in selfish indulgence; the stain upon the soul by its contempt of the rule of right; the defilement of the conscience by resisting God; all these are lost sight of. The soul's loss of its native purity, its separation from God, its incapacity for fellowship with goodness, and for participating in the joys of holiness, fail to be weighed according to their value. So, also, the penalty of the divine law, considered as an actual determination of the reigning justice of the universe, is emptied of its contents. But if the soul is understood in its true nature, with all its moral responsibilities; with its vast capacities and possibilities; with its proper dependence on God, and its accountability to Him, as the subject of an actual and righteous government; with a life before it eternal in its duration and development; the idea of sin assumes other proportions, and the peril of sin — grown to be momentous, apart from the calamitous consequences of it here, because measured by the more fearful consequences of it hereafter, when the soul will meet the judgment of God, and reap the fruit of its own doings — must awaken an anxiety which no feeble efforts can pacify. The same chord in the Christian heart will be touched which vibrated in the Saviour's bosom; and those, who in their own deliverance from the curse of sin, have experienced the might of a

Saviour's compassion, will, in like manner, have compassion upon their fellow-men, and burn with an intense desire to bring them to Christ, that they too may be saved.

No one can read the record of the apostolic ministry without finding ample illustration of these views. It is certain that the preachers who went everywhere proclaiming Jesus Christ, were penetrated with a consciousness of the reality of the coming life, and of the connection between receiving Christ and being delivered from the wrath to come, and made sure of blessedness. They preached Jesus and the Resurrection — Jesus who saved his people from their sins, and gave them a title to the inheritance. This was the energy of their earnestness. This made Paul willing to be accursed from Christ for his brethren, his kinsmen according to the flesh. He fixed his thought upon the judgment. He mastered himself, lest he should be a castaway. He looked for a building of God, a house not made with hands. He believed and therefore spake, "knowing that He which raised up the Lord Jesus, shall raise up us also by Jesus, and shall present us with you. Wherefore we labor, that whether present or absent, we may be accepted of Him."

Thoughts confined to a brief earthly existence would have prompted no such utterances. The Apostles looked with a clearer and more just scrutiny into the present and the future. They viewed, with a sort of indifference, the good and evil of the present life, so weak and diminutive, compared with the realities to be revealed. They paid no regard to personal sufferings and losses, if they could win souls. For, to them it was better to depart and be with Christ. For themselves, "they pressed towards the mark for the prize of the high calling of God in Christ Jesus," and by every act, and by all available efforts persuaded others to do the same.

These facts give the tone and complexion to their compassions, and bring them into harmony with the compassions of Christ.

We are not by reason of the preëminence of this type of compassion, to disregard the fact, that the tenderness of our Saviour made Him susceptible to all human suffering. He was touched with a feeling of our infirmities. The sensibilities of his human nature, qualified Him to perform the service of a Redeemer. He had a heart open to the cry of all forms of distress. He was anointed to preach the gospel to the poor; He was sent to heal the broken-hearted; to preach deliverance to the captives and recovery of sight to the blind; to set at liberty them that are bruised; to preach the acceptable year of the Lord. These ministries of mercy are the visible grace and ornament of his mission. They are not less appropriate and becoming in his disciples.

All Christ's servants are sent upon similar errands; and the love which is quickened in them finds expression in every exercise of human kindness. The elevation of the fallen; the relief of the wretched;

the bestowment of comfort upon the destitute, are distinct offices of Christian charity. Even the natural heart feels in some degree the appeal — though the wail of despair and misery, full often, meets only a deaf ear. The responses of humanity to suffering humanity, shed light upon the dismal regions of misery; afford glimpses of the better side of our nature — some sparkling fragments of its pristine beauty, — and intimate, that man can be something other than the enemy of his fellow.

A true manhood is fellowship with man. But this fellowship, so utterly broken by the reign of selfishness, is restored only in Christ. Without this divine regeneration, the energy of human sympathy is entirely inadequate to cope with the malignant influences which fill the world with darkness and woe. The active and systematic endeavors to ameliorate the condition of the race; to lift the crushing burdens under which men groan, and to defend them against social and natural evils, are almost entirely the outgrowth of Christianity. No endeavors of philanthropy, in any degree commensurate with the necessities of the case, have ever been developed. Christ taught the lesson of sympathy. He uttered kind words; performed kind offices; put Himself upon a level with those whom He sought to bless; put his own hand to the work and made the wretched in every phase of suffering, feel the warmth of his heart. It is for his ministers to do in like manner, with the same lowliness, and with warm and sympathetic endeavors. And this is a power in the ministry, an indispensable requisite to a symmetrical and successful prosecution of the work. It is the spiritual type of compassion, united with tenderness of sympathy, that fits for the manifold, the loving, the delicate, and the forbidding duties of Christ-like devotion.

A sinner, in the hopelessness and helplessness of his ruin, by the mere fact of his situation and exposures, becomes an object of interest. His outward circumstances do not repel or dishearten. Whether he is found dwelling amid the comforts and attractions of affluence, or in the abject wretchedness and squalor of loathsome and vicious poverty; whether within the area of neighborhood and common country, or separated by the distance and the antagonisms of half-civilized or barbaric tribes; in virtue of kindred with him, and in virtue of the unlimited offers of mercy, his necessities spontaneously excite Christian solicitude. If the commission of Christ includes the evangelization of the race, as truly as his death provides a way of life for every individual, the execution of the gracious purpose admits of no restriction to places or persons. The working of compassion must be as universal as the call for it.

A sympathy less pervasive is not the sympathy of Christ. His infinite compassions are for ruined man in all the countless varieties of his misery. His gospel is grace for the nations. His hand holds the pardons ready for sinners of all tribes, races, and conditions. His heart bounds with joy over any sinner of any complexion, or any class, when he turns to seek life; and when the followers of Christ, go forth to speak in his name, they need the same breadth of feeling, the same cosmopolitan good-will, the same lively and unexclusive affections. What else will inflame a zeal, satisfied to wait, in patient earnestness, by the side of an African kraal, for weary years, before one note of praise to the Redeemer is heard from its dark inhabitants? What else will nerve to the forbidding task, of delivering from the pollutions of the dens of city heathenism, the almost brutal victims of vicious habits? What else can enable one with meek forbearance to withstand the contumely of profane and worldly pride? What else can sustain the persistent effort to present the humble way of life in Christ, to those who by much learning are tempted to trifle with the words of Christian love? Such self-denials exceed the promptings of philanthropy. The shriveled affections of the natural heart, turned in upon itself, are not equal to the occasion. It requires the new heart given of God; the new life after Christ, and out of Christ. In his spirit, none of these things are impracticable.

It is all the more necessary to keep in view such distinctive truths now that the tendency is so decided in public speaking, in much written in books and perodicals, and in the strain of conversation, to confine religion to the relative duties, and to restrict its fruits to the courtesies and amenities of life. There are undisguised endeavors to disparage Christian doctrine, and to exalt the value of all efforts by which society is relieved of moral and social grievances. The popular religion is not submission to God, worship of his name, hope in his mercy, and fidelity to his requirements; but rather a certain cultivation and moral discipline, which gives security, peace, and convenience, in every-day relations and intercourse. It does not embrace the notion of recovery from sin or preparation for future blessedness, excepting as the latter results from uprightness and good temper. It does not propose to set man face to face with God, and establish peace with Him upon the revealed conditions of mercy.

If this is all that the regeneration of the race, and final salvation demand, the work is a very simple one. Enthusiasm for humanity, and the ordinary impulses of good feeling, are sufficient.

But is this what Christ meant when He came to save the lost? Is no more than this implied when men are warned to flee from the wrath to come? Do these things constitute the sum of the blessings, which the unparalleled love of Christ, bestows upon his followers? If so, then his ministers have no occasion to bear upon their hearts the burden of souls, or to be concerned about eternal life and eternal death. But if otherwise, if Christ's compassions moved Him to die, to redeem men from the just condemnation of sin, the weight of eternal retribution, and to secure them the joy of a heaven of infinite holiness, in the presence of God, then his ministers must be something more than moral reformers. They must strike at a deeper root of evil than mere surface irregularities, and labor to do something more than correct annoyances and inconveniences arising from transgressions. They have a different arithmetic of values to study, and a more noble end to gain. And this work cannot be done as Christ Himself did it, without a measure of the compassion which prompted Him to lay down his life to save souls from death.

If this appears to be an inordinate representation, and to force one phase of religious truth too much into the foreground, it should be remembered, that just now, this characteristic truth, by the drift of thought and opinion, and the dictation of public sentiment, is thrust far into the background. The aid of religion is acceptable for this present life, if it can smooth the roughnesses that disfigure society; if it can clothe the rude in the guise of beauty, and silence the uproar of outrageous sin. But the gospel is chiefly the offer of eternal life. While securing the peace of the undying soul it cultivates the highest and purest virtues and maintains the best moral and spiritual discipline. It treats the life that now is, and the life that is to come as parts of one whole. It seeks to form such characters here, as are fit to be transferred to the world of purity and glory hereafter. Redemption aims to rescue men from the power of sin, to excite in them the purpose and the love of holiness, and then to exalt them, justified and sanctified, to the absolute enjoyment of peace. Such is the design which the loving heart of Christ conceived, and which his life of humiliation accomplished. And such in spirit and aim is the work of his ministers.

CHAPTER VI.

ENDURING HARDNESS.

NDURING hardness may be taken to express a characteristic, comprehending the ability and disposition to meet whatever trial and heavy toil a minister may be subject to.

In the fairest view of it, this calling is noble and dignified, presenting the most exalted and worthy aims, and sustained by substantial supports and cheering hopes. It would be, nevertheless, a childish weakness, to expect it to be exempt from severe conflicts and perplexing straits. To build up righteousness in the face of domineering and time-honored iniquity, and to make head against a rebellion, strong in its vast majority, and bold by the completeness with which it enlists the pride and passions of men, cannot reasonably be esteemed an easy task. And if it is a great work, it demands, in common with all worthy undertakings, an appreciation and devotion, with forgetfulness of self and disregard of suffering, so that neither inherent difficulties, nor incidental pains, shall damp the ardor, or diminish the energy of pursuit.

To suppose that the grandest exercise of human

power, upon the most exalted plane of action, necessitates no toiling or striving, is to contradict all anticipations of reason, and all results of experience. The degree of strength and fortitude required in an enterprise, depends, not alone upon the outward obstructions to it, but as well upon the weight and true magnitude of the object itself. Great achievements involve the outlay of great energies.

That the work of redemption has this preëminent and inherent dignity is evident from the fact that it is God's chief manifestation of wisdom and love; that in its interest the course of history is designed and proceeds, and that in its development the Son of God is the chief actor. It embraces larger results and more grand than the visible creation, for that is finite and will come to an end; whereas, the glory of God in redemption is infinite, and the reign of blessedness which it sets up, is eternal. When God sent his Son into the world, in the form of a servant, He invested Him in a peculiar glory. "And the Word was made flesh and dwelt among us, and we beheld his glory, the glory of the only begotten of the Father, full of grace and truth." The Son was the appointed messenger and mediator, the representative of the Father. God glorified his Son, in appointing Him to show forth the glory of his love, and to convey pardon and eternal life to sinners; to ransom and save the lost by the sacrifice of Himself on the cross, and to bring home the countless multitudes of sons and daughters of the Lord God Almighty, who are to constitute the society of heaven, by whom God is to be forever adored, and in whom the universe will forever admire the triumphs of grace.

This redemption is but partially conceived of, when we limit it to the elevation and transcendent felicity of ransomed souls. Its brightest lustre is in the wonderful display it presents of the profound benignity of God, the unfathomable thoughts of love and mercy towards men, made actual in the incarnation; and in that highest glory ascribed to God forever, by all the moral beings who shall have witnessed, or participated in, the execution of the plan. What earth-born and earth-completed design can for a moment compare with this in solid grandeur and enduring worth. However much this redemption may surpass our powers of comprehension, in the mystery of its origin, or in the vast sweep of its effects, it is, nevertheless, the precise commission of Christ's ministry to carry it forward towards its consummation. The treasure of infinite wisdom is committed to earthen vessels, that the excellency of the power may be of God and not of us.

Christ Himself, with wonderful condescension, associates his disciples in the very spirit and glory of his mission. "The glory which thou hast given me I have given them, that they may be one even as we are one. I in them and thou in me, that they may be made perfect in one." With what significance this bestowment impresses the ministry and with what honor it invests it, is obvious. The servants of Christ are thus elected to receive and manifest, in their measure, the same love of God to men; and in the spirit of Christ to declare the words of eternal life. They are called to all the service, the tribulation and joy of this kingdom of righteousness; and it is theirs to be the subordinate messengers of heavenly mercy. They are admitted to fellowship with Christ in the toil and in the glory; not merely by their own self-consecration, but by the incorporating act and electing love of Christ Himself. In fact, a large and conspicuous portion of all that the advancement of God's kingdom demands, is laid directly upon Christ's ministers. They are the soldiers who are to be in the conflict, and meet the opposition face to face. They are the laborers who are to toil against obstructions, whatever they may be. They are to bear any obloquy, reproach, or scorn, that the world may choose to visit upon them. They are to endure the coldness and apathy of unbelief, when it turns away unmoved from the melting love of a dying Saviour. They are to rise superior, in their heart-earnestness, to the supercilious pride which stamps the cross of Christ as foolishness, and derides the offer of mercy as weakness. Where the name of Christ is cast out as evil, and the gospel rejected as an imposture, they are to stand firmly for the glorious hope, inspired by it themselves, and yet groaning in themselves under the burden of souls who choose darkness rather than light.

So far as thought can take in the issues of Christ's

mission, the fearfulness of rejecting it, the joy of its acceptance, just so far must every minister of Christ labor, with a sense of responsibility which, without the promised aid of the Spirit, would make his life an oppression and a weariness. The same grace which is mighty and merciful to save, is also mighty and merciful to sustain. He that has said, go preach my gospel, — though He has not said, no tribulation shall attend you, — has said, "Lo I am with you alway, even to the end of the world."

There is, inherent in the work, a burden to be borne and a conflict to be maintained, which imperatively demands willingness to endure, and readiness to forego ease and personal gratification and self-pleasing. The very essence of the gospel is disinterested benevolence, a desire to do good to others without regard to self. The fundamental condition of discipleship is, deny thyself, take up the cross. If it is an axiom of all worldly endeavor that no great attainment is reached without great pains and strifes, it must be still more so of this, that its success must involve toil and hardship.

To any one united by faith and love to the heart of Christ, and by tenderness and compassion sharing the woes and sorrows of humanity, there is no escape from these burdens. There is a travail of soul common to the master and servant, which cannot be satisfied, till redemption is completed; and as the Master was straitened and groaned under the load, so the servant must gird himself, and take upon him the yoke, and bear hardness.

"'Now it behooves thee thus to put off sloth,'
My Master saith, for sitting upon down
Or under quilt, one cometh not to fame,
Withouten which, whoso his life consumes,
Such vestige leaveth of himself on earth
As smoke in air or in the water flames.
And therefore raise thee up, o'ercome the anguish,
With spirit that overcometh every battle,
If with its heavy body it sink not."

If the fading chaplet of a posthumous earthly renown cannot be had without resisting sloth and ease, and meeting with resolute purpose the anguish of the battle, it is not to be expected that the incorruptible crown can be won by light effort.

The great victory of Christ, accomplished when He cried, "It is finished," was achieved, in a life of unhonored and unrewarded toil and privation, and completed, amid the darkness and ignominy of the crucifixion. How can we take up the work without also taking up the burden? How can we enter into the spirit of redemption without a sense of the woes and pains which afflicted the soul of the Son of God? How can we guage the miseries, which Christ so fully measured, without bearing, in part, the anguish of soul which He suffered? How can we follow the cross-bearer, without partaking of the enmity and reproach visited upon Him? It is enough for the servant that he be as his Master; and if He carried the griefs of a world, and sympathized in the sorrows of a race, and exposed Himself to the indignities and opposition of men, blinded and hardened in sin, with a divine patience and endur ance, with a humility as profound as his nature was exalted; it cannot be too much to expect his servants to be of a like mind, and willingly to do as He did. If burden bearing, self-denials, and strivings are inseparable from the work of converting the world to God, all shunning these inevitable things is shunning the cross; seeking to make light work of it is seeking to spare self, at the risk of defeating the very end proposed. It would at once annihilate the value of this endurance, if it were the endurance of self-inflicted, or invited suffering. Nothing can be farther from the true spirit of the office, or of any Christian service, than self-imposed or conventional inflictions. There is no virtue in austerities, nor in courted martyrdom.

There are, besides the great burdens and trials which of necessity belong to the promotion of God's kingdom, as the antagonist of all the evil there is in the world, and to the unwelcome task of reforming those who are the slaves of passions and appetites, abundant incidental annoyances and inconveniences. They have been over-much dwelt upon by a well meant but unfortunate sentimentalism. They have had too large a place in the attention of those entering the ministry. For the cares which invade the quiet of the parsonage, the irritations growing up within the bounds of a parish, the sometimes severe bitings of penury, and the uncomfortable straits into which ministers are cast, although real, are still comparatively unimportant. They are of like quality with vexations and perplexities, which other callings are exposed to. They should be set aside as of small concern, when compared to the great work in hand; just as the naturalist who in his zeal for science pushes his way through morasses and forests, teeming with pestilent insects and vermin, taking no heed of the smart of the sting, in the ardor with which he presses towards his desired object.

To dwell much on these things, when the kingdom of God demands energy, will not only eat out all true manhood, but as surely will destroy Christian fortitude and magnanimity. Under a just sense of the immense issue, all hinderances will be withstood, and all obstructions and repulsive circumstances will be overborne, even as the general, who best knows the dismal scenes and horrid carnage of the battle-field, through them all urges his battalions to the victory, for the prize at stake.

The ministry has its full share of joy, its full measure of delights, and as compared with other professions it receives an ample consideration in the community. It would be difficult to find any class of men happier, or to name any service in itself considered nobler or more ennobling. All the more, therefore, should those who enter upon this warfare be willing, self-sacrificing, patient, and endure hardness, as good soldiers of the Lord Jesus.

CHAPTER VII.

FAITH IN CHRIST AND THE PROMISES.

HERE must be the sustaining power and cheering influence of an expectation. This is essential everywhere. The question is, what that power and influence shall be? Even our Lord Himself looked to the recompense of reward; and He by no means leaves his servants to the depression and discouragement of unrequited toil. Hopeless labor sinks to the lowest verge of human endurance; and on the other hand, every energy, and the whole force of mind and heart, are cheerfully given to attain inviting and practicable ends. It is unjust to regard the ministry as a form of slavery; for there can be no exercise of human faculties more consonant with the highest freedom. It is equally unjust to describe it as unpaid toil; for although in the world's currency it may fail to show a satisfactory remuneration, yet even in this life it is enriched by ample enjoyments, and an income of spiritual good, more than atoning for incidental evil.

We are not, however, to look even to the best earthly encouragements as the true motive in this work. Its range is higher, and its inspiration comes from a purer source. The sufficient fountain is in Christ and the promises. While in many aspects these coalesce, they have also a distinct influence. For Christ is a personal inspiration, and imparts strength to the heart which trusts in Him. The ministry of Christ is a service of love and loyalty. It is fealty to a master who has won the heart first, and with it has carried captive the whole man. It is the outflow and expression, in which love and gratitude seek to bring honor and offerings to Him who first loved. Nothing short of an affection which gives Christ the first place can produce the essential devotion. "Lo, we have left all and followed thee;" which can only be truly said, when Christ and his kingdom have become supreme.

This is, by no means, an estimation derived from an intellectual comparison and judgment. This elevation is not reached by a supereminent act of reason, or by a cold mental intuition. It is nothing more than the common faith of a believer, made deeper, stronger, more vital and comprehensive by receiving and resting upon the Saviour, more singly and exclusively. The richness of Christian experience is a fuller consciousness of the love of Christ, and a more childlike and tender response to it. The more Jesus Christ becomes all in all to the heart — the one support and joy and hope for the present life and the life to come — the more freely and delightfully will every power of soul and body bend to his control, and we shall live to Him. "I am crucified with Christ," said the Apostle; "nevertheless I live, yet not I, but Christ liveth in me, and the life which I now live in the flesh I live by the faith of the Son of God, who loved me and gave Himself for me."

There is great force in the frequent expression of Paul, as descriptive of the believer's relation to Christ. He is said to be in Christ. So Christ is said to be in him. The believer is said to be Christ's — so Christ is said to be his. This intercommunion and mutual property are the terms of a close union and friendship, which sinks out of sight all contradiction in purpose, and all inharmonious feeling. It is a melting and fusing of all the passions and powers of the soul into one. It is no longer I that live, but Christ lives in me; and then the soul desires to know nothing but Jesus Christ and Him crucified, and to proclaim no other salvation but that by the cross, and to hold up no other redemption but that by the blood of the Lamb. Then the feeble heart craves no support but Christ strengthening it. Then the pressure of duty calls for no other helper but Christ working in us. Then the hour of tribulation demands no other comforter than Christ making his abode with us.

It is this possession of Christ as the soul's life, and this being possessed by Him which emphatically constitutes a minister of Christ. It is a relation founded exclusively upon that spiritual regeneration which attends the casting off all dependence upon self, and coming in abasement and sorrow to the foot of the cross, there to realize and receive Jesus as Prince and

Saviour. As there is no other door but this into the heart of Christ, and the present anticipation of the joys of heaven, so there is no other way into the ministry of Christ. All short of this must be defective in the warmth and glow which the sight of Christ kindles, and must lack that personal inspiration which is heartier, more fervent and effectual than any conviction. While to the consciousness it is always a living truth, that Jesus is eternal life; while the heart in its intensest gratitude thirsts to honor Christ as its hope; while the infinite yearnings of the soul are daily satisfied in Christ, — the bread which cometh down from heaven, — there will always be motive and inspiration and earnest persuasion on the part of a minister. While his faith is firm, his strength will be firm. The fluctuations of opinion, the conflicts of schools, the attractions of culture, and the dogmas of science, cannot touch this bond, which holds him to the heart of the Infinite One.

Such a personal consciousness in respect to Christ, and such reliance upon Him, will prove an antidote against the speculations, which are warily working to destroy all personality in the divine being, and, in a narrower sphere, to reduce all religion to the exact discharge of relative duty. Duty without devotion must always be cold. Ambition is passionate. The love of the world burns to a frenzy. And it is hardly possible to conceive of a force sufficiently inspiring to sustain the arduous pressure in the service of truth against error and sin, excepting one that carries with it the indescribable charm and fascination of a personal affection. The profoundest divine wisdom is manifested in making the Son of man the captain of our salvation.

It is the host under this leadership which is to conquer the world. It is his name, proclaimed by faith in it, that is to make the soul-sick whole. It is to the name of Jesus that every knee is to bow. It is to the love of Jesus that every harp in heaven is to be strung. It is at the feet of Jesus that every crown is to be cast. It is into the likeness of Jesus that every redeemed soul is to be transformed.

Equally true is it that all who are to be the heralds of salvation, in their work are to be inspired by the indwelling Christ, and to go forth, not only in his name to speak his words, but moved and animated by his Spirit, to do his will. All other motives failing; all earthly hopes disappointed; all earthly friends forsaking; earthly goods taken away; even life in jeopardy; this is still sufficient. "I can do all things through Christ which strengtheneth me." Of all the spiritual forces animating men, this of Christ in us, working both to will and to do, is at once the loftiest and most penetrated by self-abasing feelings; the purest and yet the most persistent. Though it may resemble the intense passion of soldiers for a military hero, the burning enthusiasm of revolutionary partisans for a trusted chief, the fervor and faith with which crowds press after daring adventurers, it is a rarer virtue than these, and holds the heart by a more profound and steadier affection. For although selfishness may not in this life ever be purged out entirely, in no way is it so nearly overcome as by the ascendancy of love to Christ, at once expelling every evil propensity, and exalting every pure disposition.

With such an inspiration it is more easily understood how the handful of despised disciples laid the foundation of the Christian Church, amid perils and hardships, and at the risk of life; how the martyrs resisted the frowns of despotic hatred, in sight of the fires; and how, in these later days, ministers and missionaries have patiently, and without fainting, preached Jesus Christ and Him crucified, in spite of sufferings and losses.

But there is still another element not to be overlooked. While Christ is with his servants, to uphold and cheer them by his Spirit, he holds out to them encouragement in the future. There is a recompense of reward. This, in the main, looks to the final settlement. The laborer is worthy of his hire.

If this be true of all lower worldly toil, much more is it true of the higher; for God is not a hard master. If there is some severity, and much burden in the service, the reward is commensurate. Even here fidelity finds alleviating remunerations. The fruit gathered year by year; extraordinary spiritual harvests; the growth of purity, meekness, faith, and charity in the church; the visible enlargement of the dominion of righteousness; the increase and greater skillfulness of Christian activity; the higher tone of morals; the advancing type of civilization; the improved social condition, and the wider acknowledgment of Christian principle in national life; the consciousness of doing something in all these benign movements for man, and for the kingdom of God, is a satisfaction of no ordinary moment. To be allowed of God to bring one soul to Christ is a priceless recompense. To be constituted a leader in the appointed way, of making known the truth; to be associated with all the godly in diminishing evil and increasing goodness; to be a builder together with God on the walls of the temple, the top-stone of which shall be laid with shoutings of grace unto it; this brings a revenue of pleasure, in the very days of the service, such as is looked for in vain in other avocations. So that the ministers of Christ are well provided with alleviations and joys by the way. These serve to mitigate the irksomeness, and smooth the roughnesses, so much insisted upon as inseparable from this service.

The fullness of the promise is the joy at the end of the day. It may be briefly stated as entering into the joy of the Lord. This is held out to every laborer in the vineyard. Not only shall his toil yield fruit in the blessedness of others, but he himself shall be made the recipient of the highest exaltation. For the joy into which the faithful servant is admitted, is the joy of his Lord. It is written that Christ shall see of the travail of his soul and be satisfied. This soul-travail is that unknown anguish of spirit in which He agonized for the salvation of the world. Its end is all the glory of the redeemed in the heavenly kingdom, and all the glory of God in the sight of the universe, when the vast plan of love and mercy is fully accomplished. So far as revelation helps our obscure vision, we are justified in considering the most ravishing, and the sweetest of all the pleasures around the throne of God, to be those exultations and spontaneous utterances, which express gratitude and praise for salvation by Christ. This is preëminently the consummation, the fullness of joy, the mutual satisfaction and united blessedness of the Redeemer and his saints.

To claim any participation, either in the antecedent work, or in the following glory, would be bold and guilty presumption, were it not actually the declared way of the goodness and condescension of God. Even so God teaches; and even so may those, who are in themselves utterly unworthy, be permitted to hope. "Be thou faithful unto death, and I will give thee a crown of life." If a cup of cold water will not lose its reward, God, surely, will not pass by those, in the retributions of eternity, who have borne the burden and heat of the day. Every form and degree of service will be equitably considered. To fidelity will be meted out its due portion; and those that turn many to righteousness will shine as the stars for ever and ever. They will be priests unto God and the Lamb.

Thus to share with Christ in the final glory of his

kingdom, is in itself sufficient; it is more than sufficient. No known degree and sharpness of suffering, which the preachers, defenders, and confessors of the truth have endured, are of any weight whatever in the comparison. Surely it is enough to have Christ the cheerful sustainer and strength, the present joy of the heart, and to be with Him in his glory when the end comes.

To know assuredly that Christ accepts the service; that He owns it as done for Him; that in the heavenly distribution it will find its acknowledgment; will not this obliterate every thought of pain, even though it be the pain of martyrdom, or what is heavier, the life-long struggle for Christ against a cold, relentless, and unbelieving world?

If these things are the true tone of the encouragement, and the real substance of the recompense of reward, does it not seem almost a profanation, at least a puerility, to descend from them to weigh and measure earthly emoluments, and to take the dimensions of popular favor, and gauge the dignity of social positions? It is not to be denied that, as a worldly occupation, the ministry is a vocation to be treated as other avocations are, and to be paid for as they are. And yet there is this essential difference. Ordinary engagements have, for their chief end, something temporal in their nature. They aim mainly at a present good. They have a fixed commercial value. They are the means and avenues to worldly wealth, power, or pleasure. But the ministry has a scope ranging beyond time, and involving, as its distinctive good, the blessedness of the soul in eternity. It cannot, without profanation, be made chiefly, or in any marked degree, the avenue to wealth, reputation, or worldly honor. He that preacheth the gospel should live by the gospel. But this is incidental. It is the care of the churches to provide reasonable support, and not the chief design of the minister to procure compensation. To make preaching the instrument of acquiring riches is degrading the calling. It is polluting the service of Christ. Most certainly no one can be a true soldier of the cross who enters the ministry with the questions uppermost: How much worldly good can I acquire? how much personal comfort can I secure? how much consideration can I gain? how can I make my life pass most easily? These are the elements of self-seeking, and these are the rewards of secular toil and ambition. Christ pleased not Himself. He laid down his life for the sheep; and He calls his shepherds to imitate Him in caring for the flock, and not for themselves. "Feed my sheep. Feed my lambs." If any are stumbled by the lowliness of the calling; or are afraid of the hardness of the way; or covetous of greater honor or riches than Christ offers, they have need of seeking again what are the first principles of this service; that it is a self-denying, unworldly service, is its glory and crown. Its elevation, its honor, is its union with Christ, participation with Him in the tribulation and toil, and also in the final triumph. Be it so, that Christ's ministers are often poor; often overburdened; often in conflict; often in peril, — was it not so with the Master? Be it so, that Christ's ministers are often despised, looked down upon, and made to endure the keenness of neglect, — was it not so with the Master? It is enough for the disciple that he be as his Master, and the servant as his Lord. The cause is too great; the issue too momentous; the blessings in prospect too immeasurable; the exaltation following too glorious, to allow a check and stay from the transitory inconveniences of time. Christ Himself is a present joy, and his joy is present strength for his servants; and the hereafter, who shall attempt to tell the wonders of love, the exhaustless flow of pleasures which are at God's right hand? Will not that vision be filled which shall behold the King in his glory? Will not that heart be satisfied that will be forever joined to the Lord, awaking by divine grace in his likeness?

These are some of the lineaments and qualities proper to the ministers of the gospel. They do not embrace everything. They admit, as a necessity, all the learning, the discipline, the trained skill, embraced in the various forms of culture. Religion is an intelligent service. The lips of the priest should keep knowledge. The pastors after God's own heart feed the people with knowledge and understanding. Nevertheless, invaluable and indispensable as all the helps of education are, without the spiritual basis, heart preparation, consecration, and sanctification, everything else is futile.

This age is distinguished for the fullness and variety, for the thoroughness, it may be, and the sufficiency of its courses of instruction. They are admirable, and give just occasion for lively gratitude. But they are no substitute for the graces of the Spirit, and the training of the heart in Christ-like virtues. Let there be no diminution of the former — for every attainment is valuable, and adds its amount to efficiency and endurance. Beyond all these, let there be, in the fullness of a sustaining consciousness, Christ in us and we in Christ. This will sanctify learning, and consecrate intellectual power. Without this, literature, science, eloquence, are unhallowed gifts upon the altar. Let a minister live and preach under the mighty power of the world to come; let him feel in his inmost heart the force of that eternal wealth of blessedness laid up for the faithful; let him be lifted up by the spirit of the songs of redeeming love around the throne, the notes of which surprise us even here; let him rise to the foretaste of that joy which fills to overflowing the cup of the ransomed; let him be swayed by the anticipation of beholding the final triumph of the Son of God, when the kingdom is delivered up to the Father, and God is all and in all, all enemies being put under his feet; and He will have a fullness and strength of encouragement, an inspiration of hope, and a consciousness of fellowship in the scheme of infinite goodness, powerful enough to animate and sustain him in any emergency, through which, in the service of Christ, he may be called to pass. This is true power — faith in Christ — a faith which lives and works by love; faith in the future, as determined and sure by the love of God in Christ. And of it, it may be said, as was said in another connection, " A drop of faith is far more noble than a whole sea of mere science."

Faith and love are the internal forces of a minister's life; and the objects and sources on which they depend are Christ and his word of promise. Armed with these, even in an age so material, amid utterances of skepticism so bold, with the atmosphere full of the giddy lights of human pride, and surrounded by the insolent prosperity of self-acquired wealth, the servants of Christ may be cheerful, patient, and hopeful. They will not lose their reward.

CHAPTER VIII.

THE PECULIARITY OF THE TIMES.

T is often asserted that the times are peculiar, and demand a peculiar quality of preaching. There is truth in this. No two periods in the world's development are alike, any more than youth, manhood, and old age are alike in our natural life. There is a growth of the race as well as of the individual. Forms of thought are laid aside. One degree of knowledge gives place to another. The horizon of mental view widens as man rises higher. Therefore, what once satisfied his tastes and necessities, satisfies them no longer. If this were not so, there could be no history of the race. Life would be reduced to a dead level, and the constant recurrence of the same forms of things, and the same tones of thought, would result in a wearisome monotony.

Nevertheless, it must be remembered that the changes are not radical, but superficial and relative. The fruit-bearing tree is constitutionally the same organization as the young sapling. The man is only the boy grown up. The mankind of to-day is the maturity of the early race. Two things do not change: *human nature* and *truth.* Therefore, if the end of preaching is to improve, inspire, and control the understanding and the will by the force of truth, the question is simplified. It is how? not what? The material, truth, is ever the same; but it needs to be presented with new settings, and moulded in different shapes. The iron of the mine is the substantial strength of the artisan's tool. But experience and skill enable the manufacturer to give it greater fitness, a finer polish, or a sharper edge. So with truth: it is ever strength, power — the sword of the Spirit — while it may be fashioned more aptly, wielded more adroitly, and applied more sagaciously, as a clearer understanding and more perfect discipline secure its better use.

Human nature does not change. The range and force of desires change, the objects and ends of pursuit are different at different periods, and in different nations. Beneath the ambitions of the antediluvians, the passions of the Greeks, the pride of the Romans, the rivalries of the present day, and the struggles for wealth and place which engage the actors before our eyes, there are similar susceptibilities and powers, the same elements of mind and heart. The wool, the flax, and the silk, which oriental art wove into the clothing of peasants, and the purple and fine linen of the ancient nobility, were of like growth with the material of modern fabrics. The fibre is the same; the texture differs. So the poets and heroes, the prophets and devout men of God, whose lives adorned the Jewish history, were men of the same make as ourselves, and their characters were fashioned by just such truth as still sustains spiritual life, vigor, and righteousness.

There is, then, no necessity to seek new material of truth from which to forge the weapons of spiritual warfare. It will not aid a minister to assume that he has different natures to work upon from those which were renovated by the preaching of the fathers. It is erroneous to affirm that men are not such as they formerly were. Radically and constitutionally they are just the same. The character which is to be formed by the preacher is morally and spiritually identical with that which the Apostles sought to produce. The elements of righteousness have not changed since the law was given on Sinai. The character of God, who demands our love and service, has not changed. Repentance, faith, love, obedience, are immutable. David, Paul, and Jonathan Edwards were saints by one spiritual process, and the exercise of like holy affections.

Misconceptions are common on this subject. It is too often taken for granted that piety in ancient days was a different attainment from piety now; that the principles of a godly life have altered with the change of circumstances. It is even represented and believed, that the God of the Old Testament was a different being from the God of the New, and to be differently worshipped and served. The terrors of Jehovah are sometimes depicted in such colors that compassion seems hardly to be an attribute of such a Deity.

And yet it was on Mount Sinai, the same mountain where the thunderings and the lightnings were so terrible, that God proclaimed himself the "Lord, the Lord God, merciful and gracious, long-suffering, and abundant in goodness and truth, keeping mercy for thousands, forgiving iniquity, and transgression, and sin."

Such has ever been the divine mind, and the work of God has always been one, to turn men from sin, that they might obtain pardon, and become the dutiful and loving children of our heavenly Father. Sin has not altered its character, and mercy has ever been extended to those who have confessed and forsaken their sins. The graces of a holy life, in the ancient and in the modern church, have been the sanctified affections of similar hearts, and the persuasion of prophets, apostles, and modern preachers has been addressed to men of one mould and make.

If then, the truth of God is the same from age to age, and human nature does not change; and if the end sought is the regeneration and reconstruction of human nature in its purity, by the truth; the preëminent object will be to determine how to adapt the truth to existing conditions and necessities. This is the principal point in which the character of the times bears upon the character of preaching. Preaching is to adopt the style and tone of expression of the age; to use forms of thought in harmony with existing methods; to conform to prevalent ideas of taste and culture; and to be, in all its dress and habit, a thing of to-day. By no means should the preacher chill and ex-animate the truth by casting it in the worn-out moulds of other days. It is as unwise to insist upon composing a sermon after the pattern of the homilies of Chrysostom, as it would be to insist upon arraying ourselves in the garments of the Apostles. Truth, though in itself immutable, comes into new relations. Life, with unchanging moral elements, is presented under new conditions. Manners, customs, modes of speech are ever varying. The substance of a temptation is always the same, while the art of the tempter is as manifold as the phases of life. In this lies the difficulty of the preacher's task. He must adapt his method to existing conditions and tastes of society; fit his warning to present temptations; admonish men of sins to which they are exposed; defend and promote living interests and issues; and urge such duties, and according to such rules as are of daily requirement. John Knox and John Howe were earnest and powerful preachers — great lights in their age. But it would be a solecism, because an anachronism, to insist upon doing the urgent work of our times by reproducing the bold, impassioned utterances of the one, or the stately, exhaustive discussions of the other. As well might statesmen and lawyers read the speeches of Demosthenes, or the arguments of Cicero, to gain their causes in the senate chamber or the court-room. All that is required, in what is so much talked of, in respect to the peculiarity of the age, is found in the exercise of good common sense. The truth is given. The object to be gained is very plain. Let the most simple and effective measures be adopted to bring living, appreciable truth into the warmest contact with living, throbbing hearts. That is the sum of it. These considerations do not infringe upon the substance of a minister's work, or in any wise conflict with its essential spirit. No less fervor or zeal, no less love and faith, no less self-denial and devotion, no less patience and endurance, are requisite in one age than in another. If it were possible to possess all the prophetic fire and the apostolic inspiration, they would not exceed the demands of the service. If St. Bernard were to arise to preach a new crusade, although he would be obliged to alter his mode of address, and work upon the hearts of the multitude by new excitants, he would find no occasion to abate a whit of that saintly fervor by which he set all Europe in a blaze.

The inward heart of God's ministers in all ages burns with the same fire, and the intensity of their effort is for an unchanging object. Reformers now do not need Luther's harness with which to go into the fight, but they do need an equally absorbing devotion to Christ and as courageous a faith. There is no foundation for the assumption that the work of God is widely diverse now from what it has been in other times. It must be in its fundamental qualities, and in its aims, the same, or else the kingdom of God is itself different, and the moral principles of God's government are different. This is not so. "There are differences of administrations, but the same Lord. There are diversities of operations, but it is the same God which worketh all in all. One Lord, one faith, one baptism, one God, and Father of all, who is above all, and through all, and in you all."

How unlike in intellectual gifts and in methods were Paul and John, and yet what positive harmony in the tone of their love, in the object of their desire, and in the victory for which they contended. Whitefield and John Wesley stand in modern times among the brightest lights in evangelical history. With intensity and fervor, with self-denial and laboriousness, with earnestness and perseverance beyond all praise, they urged the necessity of salvation by the cross of Christ alone. They preached with all boldness the gospel of the grace of God as the one hope of life, and yet they were not altogether in agreement as to the means and methods to be used. One clung pertinaciously to the Calvinistic form of doctrine, and the other as tenaciously adhered to the looser Arminian. They had no antagonism of purpose. It was a difference of understanding in regard to what the ends of the kingdom of righteousness and peace required.

To be of like spirit with the holy men of all ages, to be inflamed with the same love, to be animated with loyalty to the one Lord, and to strive to fill up the company who will in the end unite in ascribing salvation to Him, these are the harmonies that distinguish all the servants of Christ whenever and wherever they serve Him. The contrasts and disparities are only changes on the outer surface, differences of administration, and not of substance or of spirit.

The only question of practical moment is how the minister shall adapt his method so as to do the work to which in his day he is called. He is to look mainly to the end for which the truth is given. If by it man is to be elevated to a higher plane of spiritual life, brought near to God in faith, love, and service, and prepared for the felicity of the divine presence, it is a felony to descend from this high and holy discipline merely to gratify the vicious caprices of the times, and please the lower sentiments which chance to crave indulgence. Variety and uniformity are valuable only just so far as they are means and instruments for the better security of the great object. Food has its worth in the supply it furnishes to a bodily necessity. The way of dressing it, and the ceremonies in serving it, are incidental, and of little consequence beyond the part they play in stimulating the appetite so that the nutriment shall be received. The displays at a feast are tantalizing and pernicious if the guests are not nourished. And so the administration of truth, if it does not feed the hungry soul and bring water to the thirsty, and so strengthen for the conflict and duty of life, and for the glorious destiny foreshadowed in revelation, is absurd and abortive, whatever may be its beauty and polish, the charms with which it is invested, or the art and eloquence with which it is uttered.

The downright earnestness of a heart glowing with zeal for God and love to man will scarcely fail to use truth powerfully, though often its methods may be defective. The single aim to force an entrance for the truth through all obstructions to the very citadel, or to insinuate it by every honest art of persuasion, will generally succeed. The intense desire and the strong will are inventive, and they will ordinarily strike out practicable paths so as to go straight on to the mark. Under the inspiration of such a spirit, the adaptation will be quite sure to be readily found.

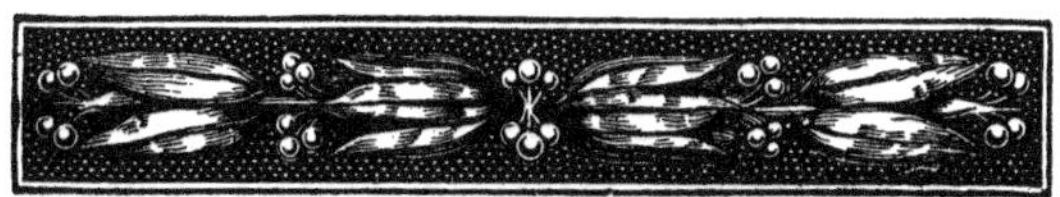

CHAPTER IX.

THE INTELLECTUAL ACTIVITY OF THE AGE.

HE great mental activity of the age is reckoned adverse to the successful and agreeable pursuit of the preacher's calling. Whether it be so or not depends upon the light in which it is viewed, and the attitude which is taken towards it. The strong tendency of thought towards particular subjects is liable to amount to preöccupation of the mind, and its absolute engrossment to the exclusion of other things. A competition and rivalry are excited, enthusiasm is kindled, devotion becomes ardent, the value of the object and kindred ones is exaggerated, and other fields of thought are treated with comparative disregard.

It cannot be denied that just now there is an extraordinary devotion to the natural sciences, and to the determination of useful results in the applications of science. So rapid and startling is the accumulation of facts, and so bold and aggressive are the theories advanced, that science, instead of imparting the most settled and trustworthy knowledge, which is its true mission, seems to be flooding the world with corruscations which dazzle where they should illuminate, and fascinate where they ought to instruct.

The process in this, as in other departments of thought, is rather revolutionary than constructive, — preparatory to results rather than formative. On all sides there is thinking, questioning, investigating, challenging old opinions, disturbing received theories and methods, a seeming demand for first principles and axioms in all the realm of knowledge.

In reference to such a condition, two things are to be observed. *First,* That a state of activity and agitation is to a resolute mind to be preferred to a condition of torpor, and an unquestioning submission to tradition and authority. No condition is more hopeless than the lethargy of mind which sleepily accepts things as they are, happy to be relieved of the necessity of summoning the moral sense to a decision upon their rightness or wrongness. The apathy and congealed immobility of a people where worship is a sacred tradition, and the creed a never to be questioned symbol of the true faith, is as hostile to all endeavors in promoting religion as the sullen and stupid inertia of barbarism. Where the mental activity of society is limited to the maintenance of a fixed circle of opinions in politics and education, and to a servile repetition of antiquated processes in the arts and industries of life, innovations of all sorts are resisted, and the force of religious truth is neutralized by the hereditary control of established ideas. Not so where thought is free, and the mind of the community is roused and on the alert. A calm sea, ruffled by no breeze, not only leaves the sails of commerce hanging listlessly by the mast, but fills itself with broods of disgusting living creatures. The wind that raises the waves not only speeds the mariner on his voyage, but brings health and purity on its wings.

The motion of the mind involves inquisitiveness, sensitiveness, and susceptibility. Break up the old fallows, and the scattered seed will root and grow. Break up old traditions, and there is room for new thought. Something good may be disturbed by the agitation, but possibly more that is bad — the despotic, the conventional, the hereditary fallacies. The commotion loosens the hold of evil, because it loosens everything. The innovation challenges the good, because it challenges everything. In the crucible prejudices melt off, but truth stands the fire. Conceits that have deceived vanish in the heat, but principles come out, like gold from the furnace, all the brighter for the trial.

In times when the mind of the community is awakened to inquire and investigate, and is stimulated to more and more various thinking, its receptivity, its docility, and its power of assimilation are in a favorable condition to be strengthened. While the mass of disengaged elements is convulsed and clashing, then is precisely the time to effect new combinations by such forces as will reassort the disturbed particles according to their true affinities. Truth needs but to assert itself wisely and firmly at such periods to secure a hearing. It needs to be uttered, not with human authority, nor with the pride of exulting science, but with that power inherent in humility when the reverent mind is itself standing in awe, and proclaims the eternal Word, in its own name, and in the name of the Almighty.

Such periods are seed times. They stand in history as formative periods. They are not to be deprecated or dreaded, but to be used. If any one asks for an illustration, let him read the history of New England for the fifteen years preceding the Declaration of Independence, and he will see how the convulsions of the times led to discussions and deep searchings after political principles and the foundations of civil rights, from which sprung the first of great republics. He will see that against the warm currents of affection, and the cherished loyalty towards the institutions of Old England, the force of reason and the tide of argument carried the people away from their moorings, and brought them happily and unitedly to settle under new and better auspices. Few, if any, parallels can be adduced presenting a more general and profound thoughtfulness, on topics of public welfare, both moral and civil, than this; and the excitements which provoked conflicts of opinion were really the occasions which made the great political enfranchisement possible. So that it is not to be at all concluded that an age like this, when the public mind is all astir, and the fervor of thought seems almost to reach a self-impelled frenzy, is a season unfavorable to the demands and the determinations of truth. The aspect may be, at the first glance, forbidding. A closer inspection renders it inviting. *Secondly*, It is palpable that religious truth in the midst of apparently adverse excitement is receiving, and must receive, more than ordinary attention. Every discussion of the day touches somewhere upon that circle which incloses religious ideas. Whatever the intention or desire may be, religion cannot be kept out of public discussion. It forces itself upon the attention everywhere. Those who assume the boldest hostility to it are unceasingly mingling it in their conversations and their writings. Speculations, assertions, inquiries, and denials abound in all the current literature. Pamphlets, magazines, and the daily press reflect the tone and temper of the times, and constantly contain references to the great questions properly belonging to the domain of theology. The necessity has gone by which once compelled religious men to call public attention to these topics. They are now either for disputation, for criticism, for condemnation, for comparison, or for inculcation among the most common themes. The leading minds — the so-called "foremost thinkers" — are by a sort of necessity drawn into this sphere of thought, and think they must; and they do not fail to give utterance to their thoughts; not indeed because this is peculiarly a believing age; not indeed because it is devout and reverential, but rather that it is a time when the authority of the past, the influence of great names, and even credence in the Word of God, are sensibly shaken.

This unsettling of foundations, and discrediting of trusted opinions, is itself a cause of restlessness. The mind has its laws as well as matter. There is an equilibrium in the one as well as in the other, depending on fixed conditions. Disturb the mental condition and rest is destroyed; and by the inherent instincts of our nature there must be an effort to regain the repose. Whatever may be the infidelity and cold irreligiousness of the world, there is that in the soul of man which yearns after something which can only be satisfied by the knowledge of God. Give the soul liberty from the oppression of false restraints, and it will as surely struggle towards this summit as water, when free to obey its law, will rise to the height of the fountain.

There are dangers connected with such revolutions, but there is a promise in them as well. When society swings loose from the authority of revered opinions, it is uncertain where it may settle, and also uncertain what trustworthy bulwarks may be leveled in the movement. But this is true: that so far as the mind has been released from servile or superstitious reliance upon authority, upon tradition, upon the unintelligent conformity to mere dogmas, it is in a more healthful state for the reception of knowledge and belief of the truth, which frames the life in godliness. Manifold mischiefs may indeed be brewing in this fermentation of the public mind; but at all events there is wakefulness, inquiry, impressibility. Any earnest thinker and warm-hearted advocate can get a hearing. All ears are open; all eyes are straining. There are wonders in the heavens above, and in the earth beneath, and in the waters that are under the earth. In the whirl and displacement, effects may be severed from their causes; and on the other side, those things may be joined which have no part together. In such emergencies, history warrants the belief that the readjustment will come if the masters of truth are faithful to their calling.

There is nothing so indestructible as truth. It may be buried, it may be obscured, it may be restricted and hindered, but in all great upheavals the perishable is lost, and the truth survives. No violent onset has ever yet been made upon religion which did not result in some signal advantage to it and to a firmer establishment of its power. No reformations have been complete, or have proceeded through any long periods, because of the easily wasting strength of the friends of truth, and the facility with which they suffer her simplicity to be incumbered by selfish accretions. For a little while the hosts fight heroically, but shortly they turn aside to quarrel over a division of spoils.

From such views as these, if they are correct, it will be seen that there is no occasion for discouragement in the current thought and in the mental activity of the times. On the whole, no one could ask for more favorable conditions under which to advocate and press the claims of religion; therefore this state of things involves some necessities and privileges worthy of consideration.

CHAPTER X.

OBLIGATIONS.

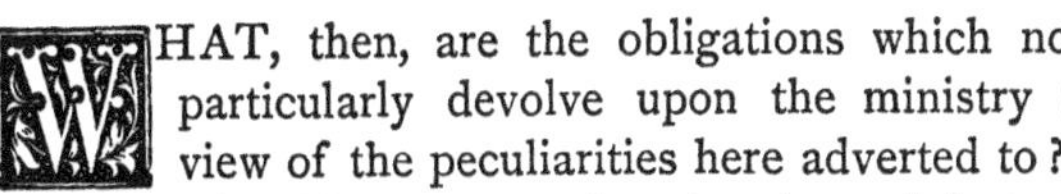

WHAT, then, are the obligations which now particularly devolve upon the ministry in view of the peculiarities here adverted to? Unquestionably one apprehension is, and that not altogether a groundless one, that the ministry will succumb to the popular dictation, and suffer its true spirit to be restrained injuriously by the prevailing spirit. This is at least conceivable, for there are few human hearts unsusceptible to the impressions of flattery, to the seductions of favor, or to the more self-originated yearnings of ambition. The desire to go with wind and tide is no exclusive passion of the ministry; nevertheless, it must be acknowledged among the hurtful influences to which ministers are exposed.

Against such deflecting and neutralizing forces the utmost resistance should be interposed. The humble but firm and determined purpose of the ministry should be not to follow after the spirit of the age, not vainly to contend against currents which have a necessary and irresistible set, but in the higher spirit of truth, and of Christ who came to bear witness to the truth, to turn the mental activity and thoughtfulness of the times towards the solid principles established of God for human welfare and the advancement of the race. "The most powerful and living preachers and writers have ever been those who, full of the spirit of their own age, have felt a calling and a yearning to bring that spirit into subjection, and to set it at one with the spirit of Christ."

This felicitous result is gained, not so much by conflict, as by control. There is no occasion for timid apprehension. The foundations are not overthrown, neither will they be undermined. Courage is needed, but not of the boastful sort. Loud declamations, hasty assertions, intemperate denials, arrogance, and empty conceits are a vain reliance. To asperse the characters and motives of those who seem to be disparaging revelation, and endeavoring to substitute some form of philosophy, some absolute science, some dreary scheme of moral freedom in its place; to charge with insincerity or with malice such as claim to be searching into the reason and foundation of things, can never be wise or helpful. While it is unpardonable to be ignorant of what is doing, and of the direction in which the tide is setting, the ministry and the church ought, of right, to stand composedly upon the firm ground which revelation furnishes, to stand there with watchfulness and confidence, observing with discriminating and impartial eye the tendencies and necessities of society, and studying with a prayerful spirit to know how to apply God's truth, so that it shall be the guide and salvation of the multitude. To hold themselves aloof in solemn awe, or in the ill-concealed assumption of a superior goodness; to utter rebukes and denunciations with oracular complacency, is poor philanthropy, and worse piety.

No minister should temporize or utter the truth as if ashamed of it, because it is scoffed at or questioned. It is God's power, and just as much man's necessity. Controversy is not the requisite. If conflict comes, it should be the unavoidable conflict to which God's truth is always exposed, from the pride of opinion, or the superficial misconstructions of those who do not discern its glory. That glory is largely in its spirit and its fruits.

It has been recently said, by an admirer of Voltaire, that he never contended against the religion of the Sermon on the Mount. Whether this be so or not, it cannot be questioned, that very much of the embittered virulence of the attacks upon Christianity has been generated by the arrogance of ecclesiastics, and the usurped authority of those who have chosen to command rather than to teach, and have forgotten to draw by the inspirations of deeds of loving kindness and tender mercy.

The qualifications of the ministry, presented in the foregoing pages, are eminently appropriate in this particular exigency. To move men aright who are already excited, they must be moved considerately.

What power is there in the service of the truth more effective than the humility which realizes how lofty and holy truth is, and how majestic and august the God of truth is? What might like the might of meekness, which, with deep self-distrust, is conscious, of its common inheritance of frailty, and, at the same time, rests with profound confidence on the help which God offers? Neither humility nor meekness are inconsistent with knowledge, with earnestness, with activity, and persistent effort. They are rather the very ground-work and essence of all that is best, and most effective in knowledge and effort, since they, more than anything else, eradicate that hurtful self-reliance which springs from pride, and which always disparages the inherent might of truth.

The servant of the Lord must not strive; the Master did not; but into the minds blinded by bigoted instructions, and sore from the burden of grievous exactions, He quietly, and with a majestic calmness of spirit, unceasingly instilled the precepts of a heavenly wisdom, and the cheering light of a wonderful grace. The common people gladly received the counsels and promises, which, though they fell to them as gently as the dew from heaven, were in fact the repositories of a power, which, in its normal development, was to raise them from under their oppressions, and in due time to encircle the earth with peace and joy. And why should not the servants of Christ, in the humble confidence that is ever the might of his own word, go on, casting the heavenly wisdom into the currents of thought, there to exert its purifying and elevating influence? Why should not faith in the truth, as Christ's instrument, inspire every minister with that calm patience, which is an unyielding firmness, derived from a source which the world knows not of? If Christ is what He declares Himself to be to his followers; if his word is that eternal and incorruptible truth against which not even the powers of darkness shall prevail; if it has in it the charm before which error shall vanish, and the clear light which will finally irradiate all intellects and warm all hearts, why should not believers, without fearing, or apologizing, or time-serving, use this instrument of their final victory? Why should they not, with the confidence of hope, utter their message; with all persistency, vigor, and clearness, declare God's Word even where unbelief, or skepticism, or worldly dogmatism, or hardened indifference seem to bid it defiance, or, in advance of a hearing, pronounce it foolishness?

Truth is not less likely to prevail because of the excited condition of the public mind on all questions relating to man and his destiny. Paul did not refrain from disclosing the strange doctrine of the living and true God on Mars Hill, because of the intense speculative tendency of those Greek sages, who were on the tiptoe for novelties, and ever alive with questionings and quibbles. He was not daunted, but rather inspired, by the presence of a philosophy so inquisitive and subtle; and braving, in the elevated assurance of a truer and nobler belief, the searching looks and the cynical contempt of the proud assembly, told them of the God who made heaven and earth, whom they ignorantly worshipped. May not the Creator and the Redeemer now be introduced to the thought of unbelievers; and while the search is going on for a maker of the world, or a method by which the fact of the world may be accounted for without a maker, may not the learned and the unlearned be taught concerning Him whom they are seeking in darkness?

Those who began the regeneration of society at Jerusalem, where there were no idols, advanced from thence to the centres of intellect, the emporiums of commerce, the seats of the arts, and to the very strongholds of the deceiving systems, which were blinding men in perdition. Their way was the very obvious and simple one, of putting the truth of God into the minds of men, antagonistic as it was to all their cherished opinions, and leaving that truth to work its mighty results under the influence of reason and of conscience, the force of pressing necessities, and the power of the Spirit of God.

It may be asked, what is there to hinder now? Why should not those who hold the truth of God, and who rest with sustaining confidence upon Christ, as the inspiring energy of his own word, by all means present that word to the attention of men, however violent their opposition, however crowded or preoccupied their thoughts may be? Is not that word as a fire? Is it not penetrating? Is it not persuasive? Is it not such an illuminator as to make differences clear, and to separate the precious from the vile? Does it not discern the thoughts and intents of the heart? Has it not reason on its side? Does it not touch the conscience? Does it not offer soothing alleviations to the weary heart, and entice, by the spirit of peace and joy which it breathes, the perplexed and the heavy laden to come and rest?

With such munitions and towers of strength as Christ's ministers possess, they, of all men, have no occasion to be faint-hearted. Why tremble before the giants? Are they not fabulous? And if real, are they not vanquished by a smooth pebble from the brook?

There should be no shrinking from Christ's work for any of the hinderances with which the age is thought to be incumbered. With all the more ardor should the champions enter the lists. The field is attractive, by everywhere present signs of life. It is of all days the very day in which to put on the harness, and, with cheerful hope, to go forth in the name of the Lord. His work must not be done deceitfully. A trembling heart, a timid utterance, a shame-faced bearing, are unfit for the occasion. It needs rather the settled convictions, the heart-sustaining faith, the all-inspiring love of souls, the uplifting fellowship with Christ, the prophetic assurance of the ultimate triumph, all of which enter into that calm and patient working, which is power.

Neither the ministry nor the church can be true to

Christ if they avoid the issue. If they meet it as in the eye of the Master, feeling the power of his spirit, reaching forward to the glorious disclosures of the hereafter, they cannot but rejoice if they are accounted worthy to take part in the great conflict. Christendom is now only a name; it is to be an inheritance. The new Jerusalem is to come down from God out of heaven, prepared as a bride adorned for her husband; and a redeemed race is to glorify the Lord of the whole earth in all the abodes of men. Nature and art, science and skill, the best products of the intellect, the purest creations of imagination, the wealth of industry and the power of labor, are yet to be the ministers of God, and to be amongst men the voices of his love. This false array against God, this perversion of the tokens and gifts of his wisdom, and of the signs of his goodness, will come to an end, and that, too, by the subduing and elevating spirit of the gospel, proclaimed in the name of God. To doubt and hesitate in discharging the duties of the great commission, is only to retard the coming of the promised triumph.

CHAPTER XI.

THE BROAD VIEW.

 WIDER field than civilized society claims attention. Hitherto the gospel, as a converting and regenerating power, has been restricted to very narrow territorial limits. By retarded steps it has been working its way upward to a more commanding position, and by a slow process, like the hidden leaven, it has been permeating and purifying larger masses of mankind. Within the area of its recognized possession and its partial dominion, nearly all its spiritual forces are expended. So that, by a sort of conventional limitation, the ministry means the company of pastors and teachers who carry on the work of the Lord, where churches are established, or at most, in parts adjacent. Treatises defining clerical duties and qualifications, in the main, describe what appertains to this class of men.

There is a broader view. The field is the world. The earth is to be filled with the knowledge of God. The good tidings of great joy are to all people. All nations are to be evangelized. A portion of the heralds are denominated ministers ; another portion missionaries. The distinction is convenient, but superficial. In quality, in temper, in aim, in heart, they should all be one.

In this view, instead of the spirit of the times, the truer consideration is, the state of the world. If all around among Christianized peoples, there is a condition of affairs and an attitude of mind inviting attention, and inspiring the most hopeful anticipations, what shall be said of the nations upon whose vast borders the gospel has hardly made an indentation, and over whose teeming millions night, relieved by scarcely the twinkle of a star, reigns unbroken? The commission covers this region of dense darkness. Mercy is prepared for these lost tribes, these benighted wanderers. Christendom is not mankind, but a fragment. The human family is divided, but the huge majority are aliens in a strange land, where they hear not the Father's voice, and no sweet invitations of love call them to his open arms.

But the Son has come, and his word still resounds through all the camps of Israel. "Go ye, therefore, and teach (make disciples of) all nations, baptizing them in the name of the Father, and of the Son, and of the Holy Ghost." To confine the work of the ministry to the narrow section now evangelized, is restricting the great commission, and contracting the breadth of the blessing. All the land is to be possessed; and the command to go forward was never emphasized so deeply by concurrent circumstances as now.

Within the memory of those living, nearly all the

pagan world was closely barred against the gospel. How greatly changed the aspect! One nation after another has become accessible. The most inveterate heathenism has yielded. The fierceness of perpetual war, and the thirst for human blood, have given place to the purity and brotherhood inculcated by Christianity. Degrading superstitions have been exploded, and the vast systems of false religion, hoary with length of years, and supreme by immemorial usage, are everywhere showing signs of decay. The heralds may now publish salvation by Christ in any nation.

In these encouraging changes the spirit of the age has been coöperating with the gospel; perhaps, more correctly, has been the pioneer, opening paths by which Christianity may enter those empires which were hermetically sealed against foreign intrusion. It is impossible to keep the thoughts away from the two great semi-civilized nations, whose relations to the rest of the world have been so remarkably modified. Every reader is familiar with the almost incredible revolution going on in Japan, and with the auspicious omens constantly coming into view in respect to China. Breaking away from a government strengthened by centuries of despotic rule; discarding a religion in which generation after generation have lived and died; allowing an intercourse so long forbidden by the severest restrictions; inviting instruction from other nations, in literature, art, science, and even religion; proposing, of their own motion, a reconstruction of society upon foreign models, and pushing forward on all these lines of progress with energy, with a remarkable degree of wisdom and forecast, and with a commendable willingness to meet all needful costs, the Japanese present to the contemplation of the world a picture, unlike anything which the past has recorded.

But these things throw over the problem a charm, a rare fascination; lights and shadow flit across the scene, and transform it almost into fairy land; and yet, to sober thought, the future is uncertain. Who will pretend to divine it? Who will assume to say how the materials of the demolished fabric will assume new forms? Who dares prophecy what the reconstruction will be, after the dismemberment has been completed? what the allegiance will be, after the total enfranchisement of a whole heathen nation?

It hardly admits a doubt that there must ensue a conflict of interests, of passions, and of ideas. Possibly chaos and night may return, and the dawning of the true day follow another epoch of darkness. Certain it is, that already the insatiable greed of gain has showed its covetous propensities. Already has avarice made victims of those whom the feelings of humanity should have protected and helped. It can hardly but be conjectured that all the nations, like birds of prey scenting a carcass, will hover around, and each one clamor and contend for the best terms for itself.

Meantime, what is the Church to do? What are

the yearnings of the Christian heart? What are the purposes of men consecrated as soldiers of the cross? What does the spirit of Christ in all his people prompt to? May it not be asked, with some potency of solicitude, does not this state of things call for a ministry equipped in the best furnishing, cherishing the profoundest and most self-denying views of their calling; men as it were transfigured into the image of Christ, and rising up with an apostolic devotion, and saying, Lord send us!

All other considerations aside, the true hope of Japan and of China, and of other heathen nations as well, must be in the principles of the gospel. A reconstruction in some form is inevitable. Shall materialism be supreme? Shall the controlling force be avarice? Shall the powers and capacities, which discipline will enlarge and strengthen, be devoted only to the uses of this world? Shall Japan have a civilization without God, and pass from the terrible reign of superstition to the colder reign of atheism? If not, then the life-giving, elevating, hope-inspiring, transforming words of the Lord Jesus, must be allowed to do their part in forming the future.

Can it be doubted that the truth of God ought to be a factor in the result? Should there be a moment's hesitation whether it is the duty of Christians to give to these awakened minds the truth as it is in Jesus? The world will equip a host of missionaries to teach letters, and art, and sciences, and to aid in introducing all the humanizing and productive operations of modern civilization.

There is another and a weighty consideration. Japan and China must not be excluded from the problem of the age. India with its myriads, hapless Africa, and the islands of the ocean must be regarded. The foremost thinkers are tasking themselves with determining whether the universe is under the government of God, or under the reign of impersonal forces and inherent laws. Admit that this is the problem; if it is, the problem comprehends the necessities and the condition of the race. It is not whether God shall be worshipped in Britain or in New England, but shall God be known and honored by all the souls He has created in his own image, and redeemed by the blood of his Son? If Christianity is anything more than a fable, this is its mission. If its ministers are anything more than masters of empty ceremonies, this is their work. If the reign of Christ transcends in benignity all other conceptions of good, then the highest service to which the human intellect and heart can be devoted, is the extension and establishment of the kingdom of righteousness, and peace and joy in the Holy Ghost. A ministry for this age which comprehends its vocation, is a ministry fitted for this broad enterprise, and ready for the Master's work wherever the call is heard. Mankind is the object of its regard and its hope.

CHAPTER XII.

THE PRIVILEGE.

NOTHER inquiry forces itself upon the mind. Whence are to come the men who will go forward in the benign enterprise of converting the world to Christ? Neither our imagination, nor our thought, is able to comprehend the fullness of the proposition. Only He whose infinite love submitted to infinite self-denials, that He might renew into the image of the Father the lost race, and lift it to the enjoyment of unspeakable and unfading glories through eternity, can measure it. Wellnigh does the momentous truth paralyze us, as it flashes upon the mind, that the vast result hinges upon human efforts. Man is God's angel of mercy to his fellow; man is the minister of infinite good to the wretched. Humanity regenerate, and transfused with the love of the Son of Man, is the agency whereby humanity is to be lifted up to share the benediction and the presence of God the Father.

It may with propriety be asked who is sufficient for these things? No answer could be given, did not the divine condescension write the all-sufficing response, My grace is sufficient for thee. The undertaking would be as preposterous, as it has often been declared to be, by those who take counsel only of flesh and sense. But when, to the fact that man in his feebleness is ordained to this work, it is added, that he goes forth in the might of the divine Spirit to accomplish God's chosen purpose, the great mountain becomes a plain. The eyes of the lonely and timid servant are opened, and he is surrounded with chariots and horses of fire. The presence of Christ with his ministers dissipates fear, and gives strength for every emergency.

To assume the weighty responsibility of the ministry is not arrogance, if it be done under the leadings of that faith and love which are the inspiration of Christ's disciples. If the heart is penetrated and possessed by the Spirit of Christ, it will pass with spontaneous eagerness into his work. In proportion to the vigor of love and gratitude there will be a yearning to advance the glory of the Redeemer. Not always will this inward force determine those who feel it to be ministers or missionaries. The range of Christian service is wide, and its forms are manifold. There is enough in any walk of life, and with any type of fitness, to engage the energies of all who will enter the vineyard. It is the same spirit working within both to will and to do, and doing the will of God must ever be not merely the law, but the life of discipleship.

If every service to a right heart is an offering of love and a joy, it may safely be said, that the specific work of the ministry is a high privilege. As such it should be contemplated. Not must I, but may I, enter this service. If there is fitness in respect to physical and mental qualities; the adaptations of make and temperament; the requisite culture and intellectual discipline; if there are spiritual longings, promptings of heart, yearnings of soul, for usefulness; if there is a hungering and thirsting to do the will of God, and to advance the interests of his kingdom, which is the normal condition of living discipleship, the question of the ministry is reduced very much to one of circumstances and possibilities.

The desire and aim being single and sincere, it must be decided whether the work of the ministry can, under existing circumstances, be wisely and hopefully undertaken; whether it presents a more promising prospect of usefulness than other methods; whether it is more congenial, and takes hold more powerfully upon the affections; whether it commands, with a somewhat irresistible persuasion, the assent of the heart, and moves with an inspiration by it to achieve a work for the glory of God and the best welfare of men. In fine, do all these qualities and antecedents concur with a solemn conviction, and a joyful sense, that in his Providence, and by the grace of his Spirit, God is saying, This is the way; walk ye in it.

He that desireth the office of a bishop desireth a good work. Whoever stands ready to go and preach the gospel wherever God may send him, is enlisted in a noble undertaking.

From suggestions which have been already made, and from a multitude of others which will readily occur, the demand for ministers at the present day is strong and urgent. Human enterprises are pressed with unaccustomed energy. The race for wealth and honors is run with accelerated velocity. Fortunes are accumulated with magical skill. Gratifications wait upon every passion, and every fancy is fed to satiety. Devotion to learning progresses in harmony with the increase of lower accumulations. Academies and colleges are crowded with young men eager to equip themselves for the strife. The more promising business avenues are thronged with excited competitors. The lucrative and honorable professions invite the studious and the intellectual to rarer conflicts, where discipline and culture win envied laurels. The duty to carry forward the civilizing processes of the age, to develop the world's resources, and multiply its means and capacities, should not be undervalued. The command to replenish the earth and subdue it, was given of old, and has not been repealed.

But is there not a progress higher in its nature, and a more noble elevation to be attained, than such uses of faculty and power indicate? When the subject comes home to the Christian heart, and is weighed with seriousness under the light which comes to us in the revelations of God, is there not a more commanding claim presented to us, in the necessities and prospective benefits of the kingdom of Christ?

It would be an ungenerous, as well as an unjust judgment, to conclude, that the highest examples of piety, and the spiritual zeal which is inventive and fruitful in the service of religion, are found only in the ranks of the ministry. It can hardly be so; nor should it be. The vitality and efficiency of the Church is exhibited in the earnestness and energy of a multitude of Christians single-eyed, self-forgetful, consecrated, who are giving the clearest illustrations of godliness by living for Christ, while they discharge with manly fidelity every social and civil duty. Such men constitute the strength of the Church. They are the salt of the earth. They diffuse purity into the very midst of corruption, and maintain integrity in the face of the duplicity and sharp practice of the market. They demonstrate unselfishness by their high and generous aims; show what love to man is by the exercise of it; and prove what religion can do in producing true uprightness, trustworthiness, godliness, and superiority to the questionable principles of the world without going out of the world. Conspicuous are the instances in which the finest demonstration of the Spirit, and aim of the gospel, and devotion to the true welfare of society are found, in men and women, who abide in the calling in which they are called, or who elect their vocation under the force of the social circumstances in which they are placed.

When it is said that the disciples of Christ are commissioned to spread the gospel over the globe, all disciples are included; and all, within their sphere, and according to their capacity, are responsible. Much of the burden must rest upon those who have also to bear the burden of secular avocations. The world and Christ are brought face to face in this age. The conflict is more open—friends and foes are more sharply defined. The division goes down through all ranks in society. The speculations of the study and the laboratory reappear in the workshop; and boldness of aggression, laxity of opinion, and license of practice, must be openly met by the well-established integrity and clear faith of those, whose religion shapes, not their carefully settled opinions only, but their daily conduct. Hence it is, that in Christian lands a wide field is opened for earnest service on the part of all believers. Not only men of business of every description can be at work for God, but all the professions are avenues and stand-points eminently adapted to successful religious effort. While our colleges are providing highly educated minds for important posts of honor and influence, it is of incalculable moment, that those who occupy these positions should be consistent and effective Christian men. In securing the rapid advances of truth, all the working force, available from these sources, should be drawn into the service. Every disciple should be an enlisted soldier. There is something to be done over against every man's house, which will tell upon the final result.

Giving, then, all the weight to these considerations

which they deserve, it still is true that the movement for the world's redemption must have its appointed leaders. The church cannot dispense with its ministers; missionaries must be sent to the heathen. "How, then, shall they call on Him in whom they have not believed? and how shall they believe in Him of whom they have not heard? and how shall they hear without a preacher? and how shall they preach except they be sent?" And then, as if the Apostle's mind caught a new glow of inspiration as he thought of the blessedness of the mission, he adds, "How beautiful are the feet of them that preach the gospel of peace, and bring glad tidings of good things!" This is the motto emblazoned on every banner which is carried forth by the servants of the Lord. The service of Christ calls for standard-bearers. And why should not the call be answered with alacrity? why not with joy and hope? why not with gratitude? why should not the opportunity be seized as a choice favor?

CHAPTER XIII.

THE HIGHER CHOICE.

THERE are many open ways to usefulness and honor, and in them there are noble opportunities of making our life-work illustrious and beneficent. To institute a just comparison between these and the ministry, so as to exhibit clearly to the inquiring mind the grounds on which the latter claims the highest regard, is by no means easy. The standards of estimation are different. While sound motives incline to one or the other, and the results justify the decision, it is possible there may still be underlying values, inappreciable in a worldly view, which, in a truly Christian judgment, will give to the ministry the controlling choice. For in this service there is a more far-reaching, more enduring, and less selfish aim than any other. The scope of any secular calling is narrow when compared with it. The aims of statesmen are shut up to the defense and establishment of the rights, the interests, and the glory of their nation. No one has ever arisen whose thought embraced mankind. But one Washington has illuminated the rolls of history, and left a name signally unselfish, an almost spotless renown amongst men of all nations, and to be perpetuated to all time. But even he was limited in the range of his effort to his native land; to the beneficence of her institutions, and the establishment of her freedom. Authors and philosophers there have been, whose penetrating and acute minds have shot out far beyond the vision of their own age, and have been willing to wait for posterity to test their discoveries, and admire their genius. But these have been few, and in the widest sweep of their discursive thought, and in their highest flights, they were bounded by the narrow horizon of time, and sought, at best, only that transient good which alleviates the ills, or enlarges the possibilities of a temporal existence. And, besides, in almost all cases the amelioration embraces only that which is external and visible, the formal and the relative in human life. Whereas, the distinctive purpose of Christ's servants is to advance the renovation of the spirit in man; to adjust his relations to God and eternity; to subject his whole being to principles as unchangeable as the Divine Nature, and to elevate him to a happiness as lasting as his existence.

This process, in its bearings upon the temporal condition, has a profound worth. It is really the elevating and ennobling process. Whoever does Christ's work is toiling directly to restore to man both his manhood and his brotherhood. What other force excepting the spirit of Christ in the human heart, can combine in actual unity and fellowship, the hostile and hating, who, in all times, have been preying upon one another? To what region can we look and see the harmony of family ties and mutual interests? Is not selfishness in man everywhere the motive for exclusiveness? Do not cliques and clans, feuds and factions, petty tyrannies and huge despotisms, mean frauds and unscrupulous encroachments, alike rend and divide civilized and uncivilized communities? Where is the power to fuse into harmony these clashing elements? Certainly the power of government cannot do it. For governments are themselves based upon exclusiveness, and every nation is struggling to secure for itself the widest power and the greatest renown. Certainly knowledge cannot do it. For the evil is not a fruit of ignorance, and knowledge only informs the understanding. The cultivated nations have not been less selfish than the rude. A painted savage who starts on the war-path, his heart burning with hate, and his eye flashing with the fires of revenge, and returns to his village with hands reeking in blood, and his spirit exulting over the smouldering ruins of the wigwams of his enemies, excites indignation, disgust, or sadness. The Franco-Prussian war commands admiration, it may be, not only because there is a charm in valor, but from the exhibition it affords of strength of combination, power of discipline, promptitude in action, fertility of resources, and the irresistible might of mind, in armies of intelligent, thoroughly drilled, and enthusiastic soldiers, under the highest attainable military leadership. There is grandeur in the spec tacle; for it illustrates the possibilities of human energy, when developed and wisely directed.

Will any one venture to affirm that the blood-guilt, the heart-stain, of the savage is deeper than that of the imperial duelists? The nations engaged in the struggle were powers of the first rank. They represent, on the one side or the other, the refinement of learning and of art, the strength of scientific culture, well-arranged systems of schools, colleges, and universities, and the humanizing influence of knowledge upon the habits of society. If one of these nations is distinguished for the keenest and most profound thought on all speculative topics, on all theories of morals and philosophy, the other is not less noted for the polish of its manners, the elegancies of its social life, and the attractive ornaments and luxuries of its renowned metropolis. How much have all these results of education and æsthetic discipline done to subdue selfishness, to tame the ferocity of hate, to mitigate the sharpness of hostility between these neighboring peoples? Are the human sympathies, the instincts of helpfulness, the ties of brotherhood, more sacred on these high planes of civilization than in the haunts of the savage? Is avarice or ambition any less willing to gratify itself by shedding blood; or injured pride any more slow to seek revenge at the cost of human life? No doubt that these huge conflicts are planned with more deliberation, with a deeper calculation, and executed with a greater self-possession; and so, it may be, with more of what is called dignity. When the impulse and purpose are analyzed, nothing will be found to justify the verdict of conscience in their favor.

Is there anything besides accepting and obeying the precepts and spirit of our Lord Jesus Christ, that will really bring men nearer to each other in confidence and good-will? Is there even a faint prospect of human brotherhood and helpfulness in any merely worldly scheme of beneficence? If not, does it not follow that, essential as other forms of exertion are, the endeavor to instill into the heart the sentiments of the gospel, has a quality and a promise transcending every other?

It is true, that often in this service the theatre of influence is a narrow one, and the results seem very small. But it is to be remembered, that the entire work of God is made up of small services, in various times, in widely separated regions; but that all conspire to fulfill that design, which covers in its span the life of the race, and ends only in the perfection of eternity.

In this view some small achievement, reckoned with its adjuncts, and weighed in its connections, may assume grand proportions. The common estimate of greatness is fallacious, for it is scanned through a deceiving atmosphere. Eternity will rectify many mistakes. The world may not think it much to bury one's life out of sight among the degraded inhabitants of a far distant island of the ocean; to give them a written language; put the Bible into their hands; lay the foundations of the church; teach them the arts of peace and the law of love, and so raise the ignorant savage to the dignity of a man, and the enjoyment of the favor of God. Viewing such an achievement from beyond the confines of our mortal vision, may it not, then, assume grander proportions, and a truer glory? May not the Lord Himself say, "Inasmuch as ye have done it unto one of the least of these my brethren, ye have done it unto me"?

Generations to come will not easily allow the memories of such heroes to fade. The seed which they have sowed in tears, and with many hard privations, will shake, by and by, like Lebanon, and they shall be amongst men as the palm among trees, crowned with refreshing verdure. How much more will they be honored of God?

Every true-hearted minister of Christ, whatever be his position, whether in the midst of brethren who coöperate with him, or in barbarous climes and among hostile peoples, is toiling for results of this high and enduring character. He is a subject in the one everlasting kingdom. He is a builder upon the one imperishable foundation. His work, if never vindicated in this life, will be approved in the life to come. Not a nerve is strained; not a pulse beats; not an impulse is felt; not a sacrifice is made; not a pain is endured, but it is taken up into that mighty current of love which is destined to bless the whole earth with peace, and make heaven vocal with hallelujahs. Not one voice raised amid the din of the world for Immanuel will be lost. Not one laborer, however unhonored or unknown he may have been on earth, shall fail of the final exaltation.

CHAPTER XIV.

CONCLUSION.

THE future of the race, and the prospects of the nations most highly civilized, excite in all active minds an intense interest. Is the race to make advances? Are polished and cultivated peoples to enjoy the fruits of a more thorough intellectual and social development? Are the comforts and privileges of life to be expanded and held by surer safeguards? Are the boundaries of organized society, and the dominion of free and just governments, to be extended over the portions of the world still under the rule of despotism, or sunk in barbaric chaos? Are the rights of man to be held in greater respect, and the obligations of men to one another to be more faithfully performed? Are the fundamental principles of morality to become the practical rule in society, so that integrity, uprightness, truth, and honor shall be the prevailing ornaments of all conditions and classes? Are the higher virtues of fraternity and fellowship, good-will and helpfulness, to add their grace and glory to humanity? Is the true relation between God and man ever to be realized, so that men shall delight in the reverence and worship of their Father in heaven, and be satisfied with the enjoyment of his present and promised favor? Is the law of God ever to become supreme, and the reign of peace to be established on earth?

These questions cover a wide range, but they embrace nothing which does not properly belong to the possible elevation of the race. They are parts of no Utopian scheme, but commend themselves to the calmest and most conservative judgment.

If such results are possible, are they probable? Do they wait, as the growth of the oak does upon the slow unconscious steps of development, according to an inherent force following an inflexible law? or are they the hard-earned productions and accumulations of thought, feeling, will, purpose, energy, compelling an accomplishment? Is man in any sense the master of his destiny, the architect of the character, and the controller of the position of the race? If he is, — and no intelligent person cares to deny it, — then it becomes a question, What are his instruments of action? what are the powers at his command for securing effects?

One thing can hardly admit a doubt, that among the chief instruments to be used are those which educate and strengthen the moral principles, and which establish the moral and spiritual law, as a practical rule, over the will and affections. The reason of this has been adverted to in the outset of these remarks. The true dignity of man is unattainable without a full training of his moral and spiritual nature. The highest culture, and the deepest knowledge of material things without this, must leave him debased, and devoid of purity or beauty. The essential element in the real elevation of the race is virtue — virtue in its broadest and highest sense. This is a fruit of the highest truth in its power over the heart. This highest truth is God's revealed truth. This truth, to become a working force, must be believed. Its potency is developed in us, and energizes us, just in proportion to our convictions. It is for this reason that the ministry becomes the highest office of the human intellect; for it is the appointed work of the ministry to wield the truth — this mighty God-ordained instrument — for the renovation of man, and his highest and noblest advancement.

All that has been said thus far is based upon the fact that the welfare of the soul, and the dominion of righteousness and peace, depend upon the truth of God made a living force in the heart; and that this is accomplished mainly by preaching the word with the promised blessing of the Spirit.

The appeal in behalf of the ministry, is simply an appeal to educated, self-denying, benevolent men to bend their energies into this line of effort. This is the call of humanity; this is the call of God. It is according to God's purpose. He has ordained that his great design should be accomplished by human activity. It is the highest conception of the use of our powers. It brings man as an actor into the divine scheme, not as a blind force, but with the consciousness of spiritual freedom, and the joy of a loving heart. The object of this work, in the language of the Bible, is the kingdom of God — a kingdom in which God reigns, not as in nature over impassive elements, but over spiritual beings, whose obedience is free, and whose loyalty is love. The divine method has ever been to establish his sceptre over the hearts of his subjects, and then inspire the willing with zeal for his glory, and the extension of his dominion.

The only consecutive history which presents the progress of mankind, in accordance with a fixed idea, is what President Edwards denominates "The History of Redemption." It is not the history of an organization, like an empire having a territorial existence, and managed by its special officers, vested with definite powers. It is a spiritual kingdom in which God is ruling, and by his truth carrying forward his eternal purposes; and all are its subjects in any nation or age, who are, in the belief of the truth, loyal to God.

The plan of God has included human services. The old lawgiver, and the leaders who followed him; the company of the prophets and holy men; the Apostles and the ministers of the word, have constituted the unbroken line by whom God has been developing and extending this kingdom. The Spirit has touched the heart, now of one, and now of another. The inward fire has kindled the intellect, and brought the power of thought and feeling into the work. Outward providences have conspired with these spiritual ministries. The building has been going up stone by stone. One generation has fulfilled its task, and passed away; another has followed; and all have been raising the walls of the eternal temple, whose foundation is the rock Christ Jesus.

The process is to be continued. Wickedness is not always to sit in the high places of power and sway its malign sceptre over the earth. Righteousness is to be exalted, and man is to be redeemed.

The work deserves and will afford scope for the highest endowments and the best trained energies. It should have the very best men, men competent in intellect and competent in heart. There is no occasion to shrink from the service of the ministry from an apprehension that it is ignoble. Can any mortal look down upon a service in which the Son of God has gone before him? Is there any splendor of attainment, or any power of mind, too exalted to be devoted to the ends for which Christ gave his life? Is it not enough, for any aspiration, to follow such a leader in so glorious an enterprise? Humility may tremble at the venture, but it can be nothing short of pride that spurns the offer. Furthermore, there are very impressive considerations suggested by the outward aspects of the work itself. From what has been attained, and what is reasonably attainable, appeals are pressed upon us.

The urgency proceeds from the magnitude of the

enterprise. Its proportions are imposing, whether we consider the vastness of its extent or the greatness of its results. The Christianization of the world, and the salvation of the race, are the narrowest limits that can be assigned to it. The contents of this proposition can only be approximately estimated by weighing the known effects of the gospel. Can any candid observer fail to see that the degree of order, security, and welfare exhibited in the cities of this land, is an undoubted resultant of existing religious institutions? The majority, it may be, are not reached by the benign influence. A huge aggregate of depraved mind persistently resists the law of God, and revels in impious freedom. What holds in check this terrible power? On what do we rely, that it shall not roll its desolating wave over the entire community? One of two things — moral force, that disarms by changing the intention; or physical force, which is the law of the strongest. It is clearly a choice between the gospel and the bayonet. We can test our estimate of the worth of the gospel as the palladium of our safety and peace, by asking, What would be the result, if at once, in the commercial metropolis of the nation, every vestige of a religious organization should be swept away, the Bible banished, and the Sabbath abolished? Would life be endurable?

It is a common belief that the permanence of our government depends upon the virtue of the people. But virtue is not a self-growth. The centuries of experiment have failed to prove that it is a plant indigenous in the soil of the human heart. Thus far, notwithstanding its restricted limits, righteousness has been the conservative element. We owe to it our strength. But there is now within our borders a race just emancipated from a bondage which for generations has been cheating it of its birthright, and defrauding it of its opportunities. These millions, now citizens, are left intellectually ignorant, morally degraded; the victims of sensuality and superstition. Does any patriot feel willing to allow them to remain without the formative influence of knowledge, and the purifying influence of religion? Does not the dullest mind see that they would become a fatal gangrene in the state?

In respect to these views there can be no difference of opinion. The preëminence of this nation, the foundations of its order, its rapid advancement, its high civilization, rest upon its widely diffused morality; and its morality is a growth of its religious institutions.

If now the gospel is a refining and conserving power here, absolutely essential in our estimation, is it not a necessity everywhere? Can the vast tracts over which the government of Russia spreads, ever contain a population which can vie with that of the British Isles in refinement, in purity, in moral worth, in mental development, in the conditions which adorn society, without the all-pervading and elevating influence of the gospel in the hearts of its people?

Can India reach its possible manhood by any other means? Can Africa otherwise be emancipated from its ages of inhumanity and darkness?

If the gospel is the essential transforming agency, equally the hope of our own country and the hope of all nations, we can at least arrive at a comparative estimate of its importance. We have the means of knowing something of the grandeur of the enterprise of building up the kingdom of Christ.

All this may be denominated the secular view. There are more profound results. The gospel is the wisdom of God, and the power of God unto salvation. Here we touch a theme which baffles our comprehension. Feebly, at best, do we realize its depth and height. All the momentous interests of the soul in relation to eternity, turn upon the cross of Christ. He that believeth shall be saved. How shall they believe if they do not hear?

For the past few years the attention to advanced education has been rapidly intensified. Wealth, with a generosity unsurpassed, has been bestowed upon institutions of learning; funds have been liberally provided in aid of such as need assistance. Year by year the number of graduates is swelled. Churches have increased, and young men have been consecrated to God. Population spreads over the vast areas opened to industry and enterprise. The call for teachers and preachers is heard on every breeze.

But if the statements of those whose position for observation, and whose character entitle them to confidence, are to be relied upon, the demand for ministers continually outruns the supply. The response is wholly disproportionate to the necessity. Churches increase faster than the seminaries educate pastors. If, therefore, with the facilities so ample, the ranks of the home ministry are not filled, what is the prospect for the destitute nations who look to this country for help? Is not the emergency a pressing one, and the urgency as profound as the enterprise is imposing?

Is it intrusive, to urge the inquiry, upon what principle the decision is made? There are substantial reasons which justify the warmest hearted Christian disciple in withholding himself from the ministry: reasons which will stand any scrutiny, and abide any trial.

But have all those, who seem to be promising candidates for the pastoral office, weighed the subject with all the deliberation which its profound importance demands? Have they considered it, standing in sight of that cross which has filled their own souls with peace and joy? Have they weighed the question of duty when, touched with Christ's compassions, they have looked out upon the vast multitudes still sitting in the region and shadow of death, and perishing for lack of the knowledge of a Saviour? Have they taken into the account the glories of that day, when all the self-denial and love of Christ will be rewarded in the completed salvation of the redeemed? And have they anticipated the exalted joys of the faithful servants whom the Lord will admit to a share in the triumph? Have they fixed their idea of the value of the privilege of proclaiming a Saviour, after looking upon the multitudes who are venturing their souls for the fragment of this world which they may gain, and the nothing of this world which they can hold? Have they measured the risk of these infatuated myriads by that searching utterance of Christ: "What shall it profit a man if he gain the whole world and lose his own soul?"

At such moments, and in such positions, the eternal realities assume more of their inherent greatness and worth. It will seem a noble calling to be commissioned to plead with men to accept a Saviour. To stand for Christ against the world, and for man against all his spiritual enemies, will be looked upon as a great favor. A new charm will invest the privilege of leading in the cause of truth against deceiving and destroying error, and of righteousness against soul-ruining iniquity. It will be felt a satisfaction, exceeding all other satisfactions, to bear a part with Christ in lifting a fallen race out of its miseries, and spreading sunshine and rejoicing over the realms of darkness and death.

There can be no doubt how such motives will be viewed, when looked back upon in the light of eternity. When the scales fall from our eyes, and the obscuring mists of time are dissolved, the clear vision will insure a true verdict. It cannot be otherwise. When all the glory of divine love shines forth, and the redeemed are in possession of the inheritance, the consecration of a life to the kingdom of God will be acknowledged the one transcendent service. That work only will survive. The rest, however fair to earthly eyes, and precious to earthly desire, will perish. "Every man's work shall be made manifest, for the day shall declare it, because it shall be revealed by fire; and the fire shall try every man's work of what sort it is."

"Oh what, if we are Christ's,
Is earthly shame or loss?
Bright shall the crown of glory be,
When we have borne the cross.

"Keen was the trial once,
Bitter the cup of woe,
When martyred saints, baptized in blood,
Christ's sufferings shared below.

"Bright is their glory now,
Boundless their joy above,
Where, on the bosom of their God,
They rest in perfect love."

www.ingramcontent.com/pod-product-compliance
Lightning Source LLC
LaVergne TN
LVHW021422110826
845150LV00007B/2044

* 9 7 8 1 4 2 5 5 0 9 1 2 5 *